DEAR AMERICA

DEAR AMERICA

WHO'S DRIVING THE BUS?

LINDA GOUDSMIT

CONTRAPOINT PUBLISHING,
WEST BLOOMFIELD, MI

Copyright © 2011 by Linda Goudsmit

Contrapoint Publishing
West Bloomfield, MI

ISBN: 978-0-578-07814-4

Library of Congress Control Number: 2011904729

Printed in the United States of America

CONTENTS

Introduction 9

Preface 11

Thanksgiving: Civil War II:
    The War Between the Selves.................................. 13

November 25: Thought Precedes Behavior 19

November 26: Narcissism 22

November 27: Responsible Adult vs.
    Narcissistic Adult.. 26

November 28: Responsible Parent vs.
    Narcissistic Parent 29

November 29: Parent vs. Self and Parent vs. Child 35

November 30: Weakening of American Political
    and Social Structures 45

December 1: Victimization 48

December 2: State-of-Mind Considerations 51

December 3: Public Sector Responds
    to Private Sector 53

December 4: Behavior is a Choice 56

December 5: Margin Between Chronological Age
    and Psychological Development 59

December 6: Separation 62

December 7: Achieving a Civilized Society................ 66

December 8: Time-Warping 68

December 9: Psychological Development
    of a Society...71

December 10: Addictions..................................76

December 11: Divorce.......................................80

December 12: Invulnerable Children.................82

December 13: Causal Connection Between
    Childhood Trauma and Adult Destructiveness.....86

December 14: Choosing a Survival Mentality.............89

December 15: Psychological Growth.............96

December 16: Obstacles to Psychological Growth....101

December 17: Blame.......................................114

December 18: Loss and Addiction...................121

December 19: Spousal Abuse..........................134

December 20: Heredity Defense......................139

December 21: Addiction is the Hallmark of Abuse..142

December 22: Unconditional Love...................144

December 23: Responsible Leadership.............147

December 24: Narcissism is Universal.............149

Christmas: Regaining Control of the Bus.................152

December 26: Recognizing the Narcissist.................157

December 27: Appropriate Times for Regression....161

December 28: Steps for Individual Growth...............164

December 29: Halting Current Trends......................168

December 30: No Excuses...............................170

December 31: Just Say No...............................172

January 1: Choosing Life...............................177

About the Author...179

Acknowledgments..180

Index..181

To my extraordinary husband, Rob,
with whom I am completely safe
and completely in love.

INTRODUCTION

PRESENTED in *Dear America* is a straightforward philosophy of behavior that offers a useful paradigm to help us all live our lives as more rational and responsible adults. The book is a reminder that we are each individually the sum of our parts and that we are collectively a society that interacts with each of those parts.

To understand a group one must study the individuals who form that group. Society is composed of individuals whose psychological development determines the nature and quality of life in that society. To understand psychological development within a society one must look at individual patterns of behavior established in childhood that are reenacted in adulthood. The family remains the organizing principle through which early childhood learning takes place, and imitation remains the fundamental system for transferring information and forming behavior patterns in childhood. The term *parent* is used inclusively throughout this book to mean any caregiver responsible for the child, and the word *child* includes male and female. Pronouns *he* and *she*, and generic names *Johnny* and *Jenny* are used interchangeably to demonstrate that the philosophy of behavior as presented in *Dear America* is neither male nor female; it is simply human.

The question "Who's driving the bus?" seeks to identify which part of us is making our decisions at any given moment. The answer to that question determines the quality of life in our society. The paradigm shows us how we can change the bus driver to a more rational and developed part of ourselves, thereby improving life in our society.

PREFACE

THE days between Thanksgiving and New Year's have always been a time of reflection for me. The ideas in *Dear America* began as daily journal entries during that period of time. I decided to publish these ideas and preserve the personal and informal journal format so that readers could follow my thoughts and reflect on the philosophy of behavior presented as one citizen speaking to another. It is my deepest conviction that the paradigm presented in the question "Who's driving the bus?" has the power to transform our lives. The more we each individually understand our own motivations for behavior, the more we are each empowered to control our behavior, improve our lives, and enhance the nature and quality of life in our society.

CIVIL WAR II: THE WAR BETWEEN THE SELVES

DEAR America,
I am writing to express my deepest concern for the state of our union. As I reflect upon the grandeur and possibilities of our great nation, I am overcome by a feeling of profound sadness and foreboding. I sense the dividing of our country, and I know that this schism is not fomented by an enemy abroad; it is an internal battle fought within the individual citizen and an external battle fought one citizen against another. America is embroiled in a second civil war that it is unaware of and that threatens our way of life. The civil war in this country is being fought over the same issue that all great wars are fought over: *power*. But in this war, the adversaries are ourselves. Civil War II is not a race war, an economic war, or a war between states. It is a psychological battle between states of mind that will determine who has the power in our society, who is in control.

Civil War II has its beginnings in childhood. Within

each of us there exists the whole of a life's experience. We all begin as children: helpless, dependent, self-absorbed, and completely lacking boundaries. We exist in a state of fusion, unable to distinguish self from other. The task of childhood is to emerge from this state of total narcissism; the method is learning. The child slowly learns to become an adult by gradually relinquishing the total self-absorption of infancy. The child learns to identify *self* by discovering the reality of *other*. The objective is to grow up and become a responsible adult able to care for another human being so that the cycle of life can continue. The goal of learning is life; its enemy is death. Those who seek to subvert the growth process and remain eternal children choose death.

The growth process is twofold; it has a physical component and a psychological component. We all grow up physically because it takes no effort and is outside of our control. Chronological age is an uncontested, biological accomplishment. Psychological growth is another matter entirely. The demands of responsible adults trying to draw us out of the state of narcissism rage against our natural, regressive desires to remain children. We resist psychological growth. We struggle with the wish to become powerful, independent adults and the longing to remain powerless, dependent children. We demand the freedom that belongs to responsible adults, yet we are nostalgic for a time of complete dependence when we were nurtured entirely. Psychological growth is the universal challenge of childhood. Every society in the world needs its children to grow into physical and psychological adulthood in order to continue the cycle of life. Theoretically, if a society were to remain a nation of children, that society would necessarily collapse and extinguish itself. The psychological growth process is a difficult struggle, but it always involves a choice. It is impossible to become a responsible adult without choosing to relinquish the irresponsibility of childhood.

The degree to which we have emerged from our initial state of narcissism is the measure of our mental health. A state of mind is not fixed. It is constantly shifting along the growth continuum, anywhere from total, infantile narcissism to responsible adulthood, depending upon the level and stability of the individual's inner development and the strength of the external pressures challenging it. Let us imagine a single life span as a time line beginning with birth and ending in death. Let us imagine a long life with a short span in infancy and early childhood, a longer time in adolescence, and the longest stay in adulthood. Ideally, the chronological development of this life corresponds with its psychological development. From the total dependence and narcissism of infancy to the self-sufficiency and responsibility of maturity, the emotional and physical growth patterns can be recorded concurrently. The child's biological growth continues while his nature interacts with his nurture to influence his psychological growth. At any point along the time line, his psychological growth can be encouraged by positive experiences or shut down by trauma. Ideally, the nurtured infant emerges from the growth process as the nurturing adult, both physically and psychologically.

Whether an individual's lifetime is ideal or traumatic, his growth patterns and levels of functioning can be visualized as points on his growth continuum. At any given time, he can know which state of his mind is in control by identifying where he is functioning along his time line. Is he functioning like a rational adult? If so, which adult? The parent? The sibling? The businessman? The friend? Is he behaving like an adolescent? If so, which adolescent? The rebel? The adventurer? The immortal teenager? The insecure fifteen-year-old? Is he behaving like a child? If so, which child? The totally narcissistic infant? The self-absorbed two–year-old? The happy child? The uncertain child? The oppositional child? The sad, angry, frightened, or lonely child?

When the rational adult identifies a child as the state of mind that is in command at the moment, he has identified one of his inner children. An *inner child* is a psychological entity—one of the historical children who exist within each of us. We must remember that we are each the whole of our life's experience and that the children we once were continue to exist internally as parts of ourselves. Even after we reach chronological adulthood, the narcissism of childhood exists within our minds. The narcissistic, demanding two-year-old we once were persists as a state of mind. Each inner child is a mobile entity that seeks to be in control of the individual's mind. The inner child's struggle for power continues to challenge the individual's rational, adult state of mind.

Growing up psychologically is the universal challenge of human life. If we understand the growth process and the complexities of the human mind, we can be more effective in meeting the challenge. To begin with, people tend to oversimplify when evaluating a human being. We say a person is nice, good, mean, generous, or smart—all in an exceedingly broad manner. But when we understand the complicated nature of a person's mind, we realize that broad descriptions are very misleading. Each of us has many dimensions to our personality. At any given moment, we may be nice, mean, or generous. This is what accounts for the variety of impressions that many people have of a single individual. The boss's wife may consider him a delight, but his employees know him to be cruel and unfair. Which is he? He is both depending on his state of mind at the moment, whether he is husband or boss.

Imagine each person as a big yellow school bus with many seats to accommodate different moods, roles, and states of being. The bus travels along the time line that is a lifetime. It picks up new passengers as we grow and develop, each new feeling creating another traveler and each new experience adding another rider. The driver of the bus is always selected from the passengers aboard, and the passengers are constantly competing to determine who will drive. To understand how one person can perceive us in a completely different way than another, we must ask ourselves the critical question, "Who's driving the bus?" When the seats are occupied by the different roles that comprise our adult lives, the answer to the question is not too challenging. The driver is mother, father, husband, wife, boss, sister, cousin, friend, employee, or employer. The list is as long as the varying roles we each have in daily life. The complication and challenge comes when we recognize that we are each the total of our life's experience, past and present. So, also riding on the bus are the inner children of our own past. The children of our childhood are always with us: the happy child; the hurt child; the frightened, angry, timid, uncertain, inquisitive, bold, or compliant child. Perhaps an abused child, a tormented child, or a silenced, immobilized, completely-shut-down child is on the bus and we haven't seen and cannot recognize her yet. All the inner children of our past remain on the bus, and they each seek control of it. The power struggle between one's inner children against one's rational adult over who will drive the bus is the source of Civil War II. Civil War II begins as a personal, internal war and eventually finds its way into external society. First the inner child battles *self* for control, and then she battles *other*. The inner children of our minds are very egalitarian; they will struggle for control with any rational adult, our own or somebody else's. All children begin life in a natural state of total narcissism, and they do not give up this state of being without a struggle. That is why growing up is so difficult and painful. Each individual grapples with her own competing desires for growth and for regression.

Thought Precedes Behavior

THOUGHT precedes behavior. If the responsible adult relinquishes his rational state of mind to his narcissistic inner child, he will behave narcissistically. He will behave in the regressive, self-absorbed pattern that characterizes early childhood. He will be in a narcissistic state of mind. In this circumstance, it is imperative that the individual recognize that he has surrendered to the regressive demands of his inner child. If he can discipline himself to ask which state of mind is operative, he can visualize his growth continuum, identify his inner child, and respond appropriately. He can shift his state of mind from regressive, narcissistic child to responsible adult. It is an act of volition. It is a choice. The responsible individual knows that it is his responsibility to keep his most developed state of mind operative. He accepts that all of his behavior is his responsibility, regardless of his state of mind.

To be able to identify which state of mind is in

control, it is necessary to examine the nature of psychological growth. Psychological growth is accomplished through the learning process. Children learn by imitation. The learning process of childhood is rooted primarily in responsible adult role models. The breakdown of the family in America is the single biggest threat to this learning process. To grow up psychologically, children need the patient guidance of a consistent, loving, responsible adult. Unsupervised children have no role models or incentives to emerge from the natural, infantile state of narcissism. It is very instructive to watch young children interact. When a two-year-old wants to play with a toy, she grabs it. The child does not care that she has snatched it away from its rightful owner. Children do not respect property and ownership. Children live in the world of feelings and are motivated by the narcissistic principle of entitlement; if they want it, then they are necessarily entitled to it. Narcissism is an attitude. The responsibility of the adult caring for the snatcher is to guide her to the realm of reason by gently teaching her that it is wrong to nab another child's toy. The snatcher does not relinquish her loot easily. She believes that she is entitled to the toy and resents any interference with her behavior. There is no natural remorse, and the snatcher does not inherently know that what she has done is wrong. It is up to the responsible adult to teach the child right from wrong. Since it is impossible to give what one does not have and impossible to teach what one does not know, it is imperative that role models be responsible adults themselves. Without the intervention of a responsible adult, no ethical learning takes place and the snatcher continues her original narcissistic, antisocial behavior.

NARCISSISM

THE narcissism of childhood is tolerable in society because it is viewed as a temporary stage of development that exists only until the learning process is complete. When the snatcher grows up, she is expected to respect the boundaries and rights of another person as being as valid as her own. That is, we make allowances for children because they are in the process of learning; they do not "know" better. It is only within the province of childhood that such allowances are appropriate.

In adulthood, allowances constitute excuses for inexcusable behavior. The expectations for responsible behavior of an adult must necessarily be different from the expectations for the behavior of a child. Narcissism is the natural and appropriate attitude of infancy and early childhood, but it is inappropriate when one advances into adulthood.

Seeing another person's point of view is probably the most significant sign of emergence from narcissism. Only when the snatcher recognizes the child next to her as being separate from herself and equivalent to herself can she know that snatching is wrong. Acknowledging separateness is the beginning of ethical living. One must acknowledge boundaries and rights in order to respect them.

Ethical standards are not applicable in infancy and very early childhood. This is the only time in life when unconditional love is appropriate. Even so, some older children, adolescents, and even chronological adults demand unconditional love as an eternal birthright. This presents an extraordinary dilemma for the ethicist. Loving without condition requires love to continue regardless of behavior. Without any standard to define unacceptable behavior, all behaviors are necessarily acceptable. Any behavior—infidelity; spousal abuse; child abuse; emotional, physical, sexual abuse; murder—must be tolerated in the domain of unconditional love. Unconditional love is specifically an issue of behavior and exists appropriately only in infancy when inappropriate behavior is nonexistent. As the growth process continues, love and behavior are increasingly interwoven. A toddler striking a young parent is not the equivalent of an adult child striking an aged parent. The different standards for behavior are essential. A parent loving a young child regardless of his behavior is not the equivalent of an older parent loving his adult child regardless of his behavior. This distinction is relevant in any adult relationship where love is necessarily contingent upon behavior. It is irrational to separate love from behavior in adulthood. If Mr. Jones beats Mrs. Jones and their children, then the terms of unconditional love require Mrs. Jones and the children to continue loving him. The unacceptable is to be accepted. If unconditional love in adulthood is accepted as a norm in society, then loved ones are expected to accept *any* behavior. Only in infancy is the unacceptable accepted. There is no such thing as unacceptable infant behavior because no rules or limits are imposed on an infant.

As the learning process advances, the child is presented with more and more limitations to his behavior. His freedom is restricted. The more skills he acquires, the more restrictions are imposed upon him. He can walk, but he is not free to walk into the street. He can feed himself, but he is not free to feed the floor. Even his physiological needs to urinate and defecate are gradually limited and directed into a toilet. Unrestricted freedom is not appropriate, even for the young child. The imposition of restrictions results in choices for the child. The choices the child makes represent his individual contribution to his own learning process. He can either accept or reject the conditions. The acceptance of these restrictions is prerequisite for psychological maturation. A child who refuses to accept the condition of toilet training and continues to soil himself when he is ten years old is not psychologically a ten-year-old at that moment. His inner child is using the moment to assert his power—understandable for a two-year-old but problematic for a ten-year-old. Some children grow up gracefully, some grow up kicking and screaming, and some choose eternal narcissism and never grow up.

An ethical, civilized society requires responsible

adults who can abide by prescribed rules of behavior designed to be fair and respectful of the boundaries and rights of others. Civilized society requires that citizens become adults both physically and psychologically. Looking like an adult is not the same as thinking like an adult. An adult who is forty years old chronologically can be psychologically thinking like a five-year-old, a twenty-year-old, or a forty-year-old, depending upon his state of mind. Thought precedes behavior. When the forty-year-old is thinking like a five-year-old, he will behave like a five-year-old. His thinking and behavior will be characterized by the narcissism of early childhood. If one segment of society has grown physically but remains narcissistic psychologically, it necessarily will be in conflict with those chronological adults who have emerged from the psychological state of narcissism into responsible adulthood. The narcissistic adult is in conflict with the responsible adult. The internal, psychological war between states of mind—Civil War II—is manifest. Civil War II expresses itself externally in society through the behavior patterns of the narcissistic and responsible adults, respectively.

RESPONSIBLE ADULT vs. NARCISSISTIC ADULT

THE responsible adult works for what she wants. The narcissistic adult either snatches it or demands that someone provide it, usually her family or the government via social programs funded by the taxpaying, responsible adult. The narcissistic adult is as demanding as an infant. The difference between them is that what is acceptable in infancy is completely inappropriate and unacceptable in adulthood. The narcissistic adult, psychologically at war against the responsible adult, tries to dissolve the boundaries and limits in society. The narcissistic adult, like the young child, seeks to undermine any of the demands, rules, restrictions, or limits of any kind that are imposed upon her to establish order. Restrictions are anathema to the child and to the adult narcissist. Narcissism is an attitude appropriate only in infancy and early childhood. When translated into adulthood it is not only inappropriate, it is dangerous.

Observe the traffic flow at any busy intersection

on any given day to witness this phenomenon. The law-abiding, responsible adult waits in the left-turn lane, even if it takes the light three rotations before he can complete the turn. The responsible adult appreciates the value of the lives of other drivers, is conscious of the danger inherent in ignoring red lights, and accepts the restrictions of traffic laws. He is mature enough to wait. In contrast, the narcissistic adult speeds up as the light turns red. Disregarding oncoming traffic, he turns on red because he feels entitled to turn. He wants what he wants when he wants it, like any two-year-old, regardless of the consequences to himself or others. The narcissist demands immediate gratification because he is not developed enough psychologically to wait. He proceeds on the entitlement principle of infancy and early childhood, a very dangerous philosophy of life for a chronological adult. The adult narcissist's demands for an unrestricted life are in direct conflict with the laws of civilized society. The narcissist is psychologically at war with the rational adults who uphold these rules of order. The narcissist seeks to dissolve the limits of society, whereas the responsible adult seeks to preserve them.

Social change is inevitable. The narcissist, however, is not lobbying for women's rights or equal opportunity. A mature concern for the integrity of the self is not the same thing as the regressive, self-absorption of the narcissist. The narcissist seeks the total absence of restrictions. It is the failure of the responsible adult community to recognize the actual agenda of the narcissist that has resulted in their unwitting complicity in the breakdown of the social order they seek to preserve. It is inconceivable to the rational adult that the narcissist's objective is destruction; the narcissist unconsciously seeks to destroy the infrastructure of adulthood and return to the boundary-less state of unconditional acceptance of infancy. Since this does not appeal to the rational adult, he cannot fully appreciate the fervor with which the narcissist pursues this goal. Since the rational adult does not recognize the sequential breakdown of the infrastructure of civilized society, he cannot fully appreciate the danger to himself.

Narcissism is the enemy of civilized life. It is the aggressor in Civil War II and must be exposed to be overcome. The obscured nature of narcissism often makes it difficult to identify and confront. The rational adult has much greater success in identifying the inappropriate demands of his real-life children than he does in ferreting out the inappropriateness of the demands of narcissistic adults. He is especially confounded by the narcissistic demands of his own inner children.

RESPONSIBLE PARENT vs. NARCISSISTIC PARENT

SOCIETY must realize that it is time to say no to the adult narcissists among us if we are to preserve a civilized way of life in America. In the family it is sometimes difficult to say *no* to a child even when the parent is absolutely certain that it is the right thing to say. Our children charm us, con us, and in many ways manipulate us as parents, but the rational adult remembers that his job as a parent is to help his child emerge from narcissism into responsible adulthood. The challenge is to move the child from the primitive world of feelings to the developed world of reason. The parent must set limits, help the child see another's agenda, and teach the child the value of useful work so that he can become self-sufficient and live in harmony with others. The importance of the parent's role as a model for responsible behavior cannot be overstated. The responsible parent is the most valuable bulwark in the war against narcissism. Considering the overwhelming damage to society that narcissistic adults cause, it is imperative that society reevaluate its position regarding the status of responsible parents. Men and women who choose to parent their children responsibly should be admired and supported. It is detrimental to the long-range goal of society's survival to undervalue the parents' efforts. If the parent is effective, and the child grows into responsible adulthood, that parent has done her job individually and has made a substantial contribution to society's survival. The ineffectual parent is the one who loses sight of the child's self-sufficiency as the long-range goal of parenthood. If the parent surrenders to the child's narcissistic standard, the parent has relinquished her power to the child and has unwittingly helped sabotage the child's growth process. Why would any parent relinquish her power to a son or daughter? How does this happen?

To answer these questions, it is necessary to understand that the parent also begins life as a narcissistic baby engaged in a parallel power struggle with his own parents. The cyclical, multigenerational nature of this dynamic must be emphasized. In his own childhood, the parent struggled to remain a baby as his parents attempted to propel him into adulthood. The degree to which he has emerged from his own state of narcissism determines the level of responsible adulthood with which he can parent. So, remembering that no one can give what he does not have or teach what he does not know, it becomes clear that a narcissistic adult cannot be a responsible role model to his children. It is a contradiction in terms. The narcissistic parent cannot parent effectively.

If the parent has achieved a partial realization of psychological development somewhere between total narcissism and responsible adulthood, her parenting will be inconsistent. When her state of mind is adult, her parenting decisions will be rational and constructive and will favor growth and development. When her attitude is narcissistic, the parent's decisions will be emotional and destructive and will favor regression and narcissism. This parent confuses the child by displaying mixed messages about the necessity to grow up. The inconsistent, partially developed parent is unstable and particularly vulnerable to the manipulations of her children. Remember that a state of mind is not fixed; it is constantly shifting along the growth continuum from infantile narcissism to rational adulthood, depending upon its internal strength of development and the external provocation that threatens its stability. Keeping the most developed, rational, adult state of mind operative and in control is an ongoing challenge, especially for parents.

One must never underestimate the charm or intelligence of the committed narcissistic child. He is a master at psychological warfare. The parent presents the child with rational arguments. "No, Johnny, you cannot stay out until midnight on a school night. You have work to do, and you must be up at 6 AM." The child is unmoved by rational thought because he operates from the world of *feelings*. "But I want to go, Mom. Everyone will be there. Everyone else's parents are letting them go." Phase two has begun. The child has shifted the debate from rational thought to the arena of feelings. He has introduced his two favorite weapons: *guilt* and *fear.*

The well-intentioned parent wants to be a good parent. Johnny knows this and uses it to his advantage. He is also very well aware of the emotional power he wields. Johnny knows that his parents *want* his love. If they also *need* his love, the balance of power in the relationship is definitely in Johnny's favor. The difference between *want* and *need* is crucial for the parent to understand. *Want* in this circumstance derives from the rational, adult state of mind. *Need* derives from the unmet emotional needs of the parent's inner child. When the parent *wants* her child's love, she is experiencing the hope appropriate to the parent-child relationship. When the parent *needs* her child's love, the parent is attempting to remedy her own impoverished childhood with her real child. She has confused the past with the present and replaced hope with expectation. In this state of mind, the parent is particularly vulnerable to Johnny's manipulations because they mobilize her needy inner child. Johnny's reference to "everyone else's parents" is specifically designed to make his parents feel insecure and guilty. A narcissistic child resents any comparison between himself and other children, but he does not hesitate to compare his parents to "everyone else's parents" when it suits his needs. Since guilt implies wrongdoing, Johnny's maneuver goes something like this: *If I convince Mom and Dad that they made a wrong decision, then they will feel guilty and let me go.* Johnny does not know why his maneuvering works; he just knows that it does. If the parents have not said yes by now, Johnny goes in for the kill. He turns his back on his mom and storms out of the room. This particular move is designed to instill the fear of abandonment in his mother by mobilizing her inner child. If Mom needs Johnny's love, she is particularly vulnerable now. For a moment, Mom feels the pain of life without Johnny's love. If she allows her inner child to be in control of her mind, she will feel the anxiety and dread of loss. This is a critical moment. If Mom can stay firm and remember the difference between *want* and *need*, she will realize that Johnny is trying to manipulate her by provoking her inner child. She will recall that her position of strength is to remain the responsible parent, stay in the present, and ignore his invitation to regress. The responsible adult wants her child's love and admiration; the underdeveloped parent needs her child's love and approval. If Mom can resist Johnny's pressure to regress developmentally, she will be in a position of strength to confront him and refuse to surrender to his demand. She will remember the mantra of the narcissist: "I want what I want when I want it." If she holds her ground, she has won this battle of emotional blackmail, but the war continues. Conversely, if she surrenders, she has lost this battle, but since the war rages on she will have the opportunity to reassert herself tomorrow when Johnny presents her with his next narcissistic demand. One characteristic of the narcissism of childhood is that the demands are unceasing. In this forum, the parent has unlimited opportunities to improve and do better the next time. Practice makes perfect.

PARENT VS. SELF AND PARENT VS. CHILD

THE difficulty for all well-intentioned parents is clear. The war appears to be a battle between parent and child, but in reality the war has two fronts. First, there is the struggle for the parent to remain a responsible adult *internally* while under attack from his own narcissistic *inner* children. Second, there is the parallel struggle for him to remain a responsible adult *externally* while under attack from his real-life, narcissistic *outer* children. The pressure to relinquish control to his outer children is parallel to the pressure to relinquish control to his inner children. The battlefronts are first between parent and self, and second between parent and child. If the parent understands the nature of the war, he will be much better prepared to confront the inner and outer attacks on his selfness. The parent cannot succeed in the power struggle with his outer children if he has not first succeeded in controlling his inner children. To monitor his behavior, it is necessary for the parent to assess the status of the internal and external fronts of the war. He must continually ask himself the crucial question, "Who's driving the bus?" The answer will immediately give the parent the information necessary to proceed. Only when the parent recognizes that he has relinquished control of himself to one of his inner children can he regain control of the bus and reestablish his adult authority with his outer children.

The parent's position of strength is to remember three things. Number one, the external battle is not personal. This is a real challenge because it seems so personal at the time. The parent must, however, remember that the task of childhood is emotional growth and that relinquishing the state of narcissism is *always* a struggle for the child. The battle between parent and child is inevitable but not personal. Number two, the parent must remember that the child operates from the world of *feelings,* not thought. The child's power base rests on provoking feelings of guilt and fear in the parent that catapult the parent backward on the growth continuum. The parent's position of strength is to resist these attacks and stay in the world of rational thought, where her adult drives the bus. If the parent allows Johnny to draw her into the world of feelings, Johnny has engaged the parent's inner child to drive the bus where Johnny can win the battle. Johnny does not know why he is able to manipulate his parents; he just knows how to do it. His parents don't understand why they give in to Johnny; they just know it happens. Understanding the psychodynamics of their interaction with Johnny is an extremely effective way for the parents to change the pattern and regain parental control. Number three, the parent must remember that the goal of parenting is to help her children become responsible, self-sufficient adults so that the cycle of life continues and society survives. Child-raising decisions need to be evaluated on the basis of the answer to this question: "Will this decision promote adulthood or narcissism?" Decisions that lead to growth and self-sufficiency are positive. Decisions that promote the regressive return to narcissism are negative.

The good-bad dichotomy may seem simplistic, but the struggle between well-intentioned parents and their children is really simple. Parenting is a struggle for power because the child wants to remain a child and the parent wants the child to become an adult. If parents can discipline themselves to remember that this is a psychological battle for power, they will realize that physical responses are destructive, unnecessary and counterproductive.

It is unnecessary to escalate the battle by hitting, pushing, slapping, or by introducing weapons such as paddles and straps. Escalation is counterproductive because physical punishment is primitive and does not address the psychological issues that are being fought over. In the end, if the child is taught a physical response to a psychological problem, she is not being equipped to function in the world of responsible adulthood. She does not learn self-control from an out-of-control role model who pummels her. This presents a problem. What if the parent is

underdeveloped psychologically and responds auto-
matically with violence? Since no one can teach what
he does not know or give what he does not have, how
can a parent teach self-control if he responds by being
out of control himself? He can't.

The remedy for this problem begins with self-
awareness through education. In certain forms of
psychotherapy, the student can learn the techniques
required to recognize the passengers on his bus and
the skills necessary to keep his responsible, adult state
of mind in control of the bus. Mental health needs
to become our nation's conscious priority to ensure
that chronological adults are emotionally developed
enough to help their children grow up. It is imperative
for well-intentioned parents struggling to raise responsible children in a narcissistic society to constantly
be aware of who is driving the bus. The parent must
discipline herself to visualize her own time line so that
she can identify who is in control of her mind. Adult
education classes teaching parenting skills would be
extremely helpful in defining the parent's inner and
outer struggles. Teaching her techniques to identify
and cope with her own inner life would be a powerful
tool in helping the parent respond responsibly at
home. The parent must discipline herself to stay in
the position of responsible adult and not allow her son
or daughter to provoke her backward into a state of
narcissism where the likelihood that she will respond
with violence is the greatest. That is, the parent must
remain the responsible, adult role model even while
under siege by her real, narcissistic children. The

parent's inner adult state of mind must drive the bus. The parent must stay in control of her own mind. Nature will take care of the children's physical growth, but parents have the responsibility for their children's psychological growth. A parent cannot be effective while an inner child is driving the bus.

Verbal assaults on children are also unacceptable teaching methods. Being abusive in any way discourages civilized behavior in one's children because they learn by imitation. It is impossible for the child to understand the psychodynamics of his parents' behavior. It is the rare child who can even recognize early in life when his parents' behavior is wrong. This awareness usually comes later in life when the child can see for himself that not all parents behave like his parents do. If the child is lucky enough to have a positive adult role model in his life, such as a teacher or friend's parent, he may choose to pattern his own behavior after the positive role model rather than his own parents. This child will imitate the positive role model and reject the behavior of his parent. He might also decide to just do the opposite of whatever his parents do. In this primitive way, he has decided to be positive rather than negative. He has chosen life. This particular decision will put him in serious opposition to his parents, but it will serve him well in his adult life.

Unless a child is totally locked away from society and is held captive in the unsavory environment of abusive parents, that child has ample opportunity in his childhood to see positive role models. It is a serious flaw in the thinking of many of today's sociologists and psychologists that individuals are just helpless victims of their upbringings. This view is appropriate to infancy and early childhood but is seriously defective when applied to adolescence and adulthood. These well-intentioned social scientists overlook the contribution of the individual when they explain negative behavior. Their tendency to blame Mom and Dad relieves the adolescent and adult from any personal responsibility for antisocial behavior. This is a serious problem in our society since the social scientists are viewed as experts on behavior. Now we have experts who no longer demand personal responsibility for behavior. Explanations have become excuses. The experts have institutionally affirmed a return to narcissism, where there is no personal accountability. In this atmosphere, the unacceptable is accepted and the inexcusable is excused. The complicity of the social scientists in the dismantling of civilized society must be examined. How is it possible that the experts have relinquished the responsible adult position and accepted narcissism as a way of life?

Psychiatrists, psychologists, social workers, and sociologists are not a homogeneous group of one opinion. The world of mental health is experiencing the same struggle in which parents are engaged. Narcissism is an attitude. It is a point of view that is evident in every profession, including the mental health profession. The war between narcissists and responsible adults is pervasive. The battles are being staged throughout the country in homes, businesses, private offices, public institutions, courts, and schools. The narcissists promulgate their victim theories against the responsible adults who fight against excuses and demand personal responsibility for behavior. The problem is one of numbers. As our society is beset with more and more narcissistic individuals, the responsible adults are being overshadowed, overshouted, and overwhelmed. It is because of this growing population of narcissistic adults that our society is becoming increasingly out of control. Narcissistic adults occupy many positions of power in both the private and public sectors of life. Emotionally they are very underdeveloped, but intellectually they may be very high achievers and may hold enormously influential positions.

As the population of narcissists increases and gets old enough to vote, it elects officials sympathetic to the narcissists' regressive demands. They elect officials who cannot possibly deliver on promises because the promises themselves are so unrealistic. However, the narcissistic voter proceeds from the world of feelings and not the world of rational thought. He considers it a victory if his candidate wins, even though the candidate will not do what he says. Like a child, the adult narcissist evaluates political candidates on what the candidate says, not on what he does. The candidate's voting record, behavior, and personal integrity are irrelevant. The narcissist votes like a child. He is easily swayed and manipulated because he does not stay in the world of facts and evidence. Narcissists consistently elect the politician who promises to take care of them and protect them, the politician who preserves their illusion of safety. The savvy politician tells his constituency whatever makes them feel good. He appeals to their emotions, not their rational thought processes. The politician knows that the childish, magical thinking of the voters will protect him from the natural and logical consequences of public scrutiny. The adult narcissist has the power to vote, but since his perspective is that of a child, he elects candidates who encourage and represent regression rather than growth. Narcissists elect narcissists. Narcissists are particularly drawn to politicians who blame everyone else for society's ills. Blame suits the narcissist. The candidate who advocates personal responsibility and the merit system is not elected in a climate of political correctness, where feelings are more compelling than facts.

Today it is political suicide to promulgate a meritocracy where excellence rather than need determines advancement. A meritocracy is considered insensitive to the feelings of those who are passed over. It is fascinating that the double standard of the narcissist is unmistakable in this argument. Consider the situation where there is only one space for two applicants. The meritocracy demands that the more qualified candidate advance. The politically correct, need-based system of the narcissist demands that the more needy candidate advance so that his feelings will not be hurt. Since only one contender can get the job, why is it the feelings of the needier that matter most? Why are the feelings of the more qualified candidate disregarded? In the narcissist's world of feelings, it is only the narcissist's feelings that count.

The infrastructure of the narcissist is extremely fragile. It cannot withstand rational scrutiny because its ethical system protects only the narcissist. It is completely unfair. It is the "me first" philosophy of early childhood inappropriately advanced into adulthood. The narcissist rejects any serious examination of his ethical system. He has learned that his best defense is an offense, so to deflect investigation he launches a counterattack. Any candidate bold enough to question the prevailing political correctness is censured, smeared, snubbed, or denounced by his party. The narcissist is adept at provoking guilt. If the narcissist can engage the hurt inner children in society to identify with the less qualified candidate, he has successfully shifted the focus from qualifications to feelings. The climate for acceptance of regressive, need-based policies is thus established. Society feels sorry for the less-qualified candidate, sees him as a victim, and feels guilty when he does not advance. Again, the narcissistic agenda has prevailed because it has interrupted free thought, free speech, and free expression by wielding the dual whips of guilt and fear. Students, teachers, public officials, and journalists are no longer free to speak out for fear of reprisals. Students fear being failed or expelled, journalists and public officials risk being fired, professors can lose tenure, and responsible politicians risk not being reelected. The voting public feels guilty, so they support the need-based standard of advancement.

The narcissist has prevailed. The climate of guilt and fear instilled by a multitude of noisy narcissists is very destructive. If the quiet majority of responsible adults in our society do not take serious steps to stop the aggression of the adult narcissists among us, we will lose the battle for control of society. Civil War II is a very real conflict, even though most of its adversaries are unaware of its existence.

WEAKENING OF AMERICAN POLITICAL AND SOCIAL STRUCTURES

THE weakening of the American political structure by voting narcissists is augmented by the weakening of our social structure when behavior experts promulgate narcissistic victimization theories. The victimization theories of many social scientists are widely accepted in America today as excuses rather than explanations for behavior. They have infiltrated the judicial system where judges and juries repeatedly let criminals go free without paying any consequences for their behavior. Why? The answer is twofold.

First, like savvy politicians, manipulative attorneys are very well trained in how to draw judges and juries into narcissistic states of mind where the criminal is seen as a victim instead of a victimizer. Second, the narcissistic position of not taking responsibility for one's actions has been institutionalized in the insanity defense. What was conceived as a well-intentioned framework for determining the state of mind of the perpetrator at the time of a crime has deteriorated into a gigantic loophole for victimizers in today's society.

To begin with, rational, healthy individuals do not rape, torture, or murder. So what is the point of establishing the perpetrator's state of mind? Was the victimizer angry or jealous or full of rage? The questions they are asking are, "What was his state of mind? Who was driving the criminal's bus at the time of the crime?" Does it matter? I don't think so. Each individual must be responsible for every passenger on his bus. No excuses. The only reason society is sympathetic to some of the revenge crimes we witness today is that when the law has ceased to protect the innocent, law-abiding citizen, there is a certain pleasure in seeing that person take the law into his own hands. This is the attraction of *Dirty Harry* at the movies. Society would not sympathize with Dirty Harry if our institutions protected law-abiding citizens. In our upside-down society, when we accept the insanity defense, we embrace the convoluted thinking of the narcissist and the victimizer is protected at the expense of the victim. Something is seriously wrong and cannot be righted until individuals are accountable for their behaviors. No excuses.

The loophole of the insanity defense must be eliminated. Social scientists need to rethink and redefine insanity so that they do not excuse present behavior on the basis of a narcissistic state of mind rooted in the past. The experts cannot be effective in promoting growth if they adopt a regressive agenda that defends being stalled in the past. The underlying assumption of the insanity plea is that the victimizer is truly the victim because she was not in a rational state of mind at the time of the crime. This is a seriously flawed argument because it assumes that a person's state of mind is out of her control. If we are to accept this thesis, then no person can ever be held responsible for her actions because she can always contend that her angry inner child was in command. That is, she can always argue that she was not in a rational state of mind at the time of the crime. This may be useful as an *explanation* of behavior, but it must never be accepted as an *excuse* for behavior. It is imperative, if society is to be civilized, that each individual accepts responsibility for every passenger on his bus.

So, who is a victim? The victim is the unfortunate recipient of the victimizer's actions. The person who is robbed, tortured, raped, or murdered is the victim. In a civilized society, victim and victimizer are not confused. Yet in our society, these boundaries are being blurred.

VICTIMIZATION

VICTIMIZATION is a condition that has been exploited in today's society by victimizers and their advocates. The victimizer contends that since he was victimized as a child, he is not responsible for his actions today. His defense confuses the past with the present and rejects any notion of personal responsibility that comes with age. Children are truly victims. Since they have no choices, they have no power. The victimizer, however, is no longer a child, yet he demands that his behavior be assessed on the same standard as a child's. Society has declared age eighteen as the onset of adulthood. As of this date, individuals can vote and make contracts to which they are legally bound. In this way, society has declared that at age eighteen an individual is responsible for his actions. Why is this commitment to responsibility abandoned to protect a victimizer? The well-meaning social scientists have intruded on civilized society again. In their quest to provide explanations for the inexplicable, they have provided excuses for the inexcusable. When society accepts these explanations as excuses, they have collaborated with the victimizers and the social scientists to relieve the victimizer of any personal responsibility for his choices.

A chronological adult must never be confused with a chronological child. Even an underdeveloped adult is still a chronological adult after age eighteen. Many in the mental health field will argue that an underdeveloped adult is "really" a child, but this argument alters reality and is destructive to the members of society who have developed rational states of mind. It creates an unacceptable virtual reality to accommodate the psychologically underdeveloped individual. This shift to virtual reality involves a regression from the rational, adult state of mind rooted in the present to the narcissistic state of mind stalled in the past. Again, the unproductive member of society is being protected at the expense of the productive member, and the meritocracy is rejected in favor of a need-based standard of behavior. *Want* and *need* are synonymous to the narcissist. When adult Jenny steals from her neighbor, she operates on little Jenny's narcissistic principle of entitlement. "I want it, so I need it. I need it, so I will take it." If Jenny were a rational adult, she would operate on the adult principle of performance. "I want it, so I will work for it." Need is the base appropriate to infancy and early childhood; performance is the base appropriate to adolescence and adulthood. When the need-based standard of behavior inappropriately advances into adulthood and replaces the performance-based standard, it is extremely damaging to the survival of civilized society.

When society accepts virtual reality as objective reality, it accepts the past as the present.

The inner child lives in the subjective virtual reality of the past, but the chronological adult exists in real life in the present. Jenny's real-life behavior has real consequences in the present, no matter what historic state of mind motivated her choices. If a chronological adult's inexcusable behavior is excused on the basis of her state of mind at the time, then no citizen can ever be held responsible for her behavior. The state-of-mind defense removes any limits or restrictions on human behavior. The ramifications of this defense are catastrophic.

To be in touch with objective reality, it is imperative that an individual's state of mind be consistent with her existence in the present. When society accepts a chronological adult as "really" a child, there is no standard of objective reality from which to test reality. Crime does not emanate from a rational, adult state of mind; it proceeds from the inner child's narcissistic attitude of entitlement inappropriately advanced into adulthood. Accepting a chronological adult as "really" a child is accepting the subjective reality of narcissism and is extremely subversive to the growth process. Why would Jenny ever stop snatching if snatching is regarded as acceptable?

STATE-OF-MIND CONSIDERATIONS

STATE-OF-MIND considerations raise other compelling issues regarding the question, "Who is a child?" Adult crimes are being committed regularly by youths thirteen years old and sometimes as young as seven or eight. Are these children to be considered adults because of the viciousness of their crimes? Is it rational to protect a child victimizer as a child who does not know better? If they are not children, what are they? It defies common sense for society to deem a thirteen-year-old legally bound to contracts, but is it right to protect this child when he commits rape and murder? In many communities, adult criminals deliberately engage the services of thirteen-year-olds in drug deals, robberies, and murders because our society legally protects these children from the consequences of their behavior. Responsible adults become accomplices to this travesty by permitting the loophole. Juvenile offenders must be removed from society to safeguard law-abiding individuals. The recognition that juvenile offenders are chronological children would be the concession that they be housed in special facilities where they can be rigorously trained to learn new patterns of thinking that change their behavior. The infrastructure for this program already exists within the juvenile justice system, which, at present, is a failure because it is not committed to the growth process of the juvenile. Without growth there is no behavior change. Addressing this issue is a necessity. Juveniles who commit serious crimes are underdeveloped psychologically, even at their young ages. They need intensive adult supervision, guidance, and nurturing to help them emerge from their narcissism. Society must commit its resources to this effort both publicly and privately. Without a commitment to growth and objective reality, the narcissistic perspective of no limits and no rules becomes institutionalized and social chaos necessarily results.

PUBLIC SECTOR RESPONDS TO PRIVATE SECTOR

THE manner in which the public sector responds to the private sector is a reflection of the development of society. The psychological development of individual citizens parallels the mood of society. Public opinion is a matter of numbers. If most citizens function with developed, rational states of mind, the public sector responds with responsible legislation and rational programs that encourage self-sufficiency and personal responsibility for behavior. If most citizens function with underdeveloped, narcissistic states of mind, the public sector responds with legislation and programs that encourage regression, dependence, and excuses for behavior. When public opinion favors regression, society becomes more and more out of control because it allows the standards of behavior appropriate to childhood to intrude upon adulthood. It no longer distinguishes between childhood and adulthood, between past and present.

These boundaries are blurred, and both the private and public sectors impose fewer constraints upon the inner children. When the pressure to emerge from narcissism is removed, a state of chaos results. The emboldened inner child overwhelms the rational, adult state of mind, and the inner child is then free to drive the bus. When an angry inner child is driving the bus and has the weapons of adulthood at his disposal, we are witness to a juvenile delinquent or a career criminal, depending on whether the delinquent has chosen crime as a permanent lifestyle. When little Johnny grows up, *snatching* is called *stealing*. This change in description parallels the change in personal responsibility that comes with age. A two-year-old is not the same as a twelve-year-old or an eighteen-year-old. Society's mistake is in perceiving these three offenders as if they were the same.

Judges, juries, and social scientists seem to have difficulty distinguishing the roles, responsibilities, and rules appropriate to different stages of life. The biological difference is readily apparent, but the psychological difference is not as clear because it is a matter of responsibility. As the child grows up biologically, he must be held increasingly accountable for his behavior. If society sanctions unconditional acceptance of its citizens, then Johnny's stealing becomes socially accepted. If this happens, civilized life with its respect for boundaries is disvalued, and chaos—its unregulated counterpoint—is valued. The only person who benefits from unconditional acceptance is narcissistic Johnny. When society accepts the unacceptable,

Johnny is free to plunder responsible citizens. Johnny retains a court-appointed lawyer (at society's expense) to argue that he did not have a proper role model to guide him in his youth. Poor Johnny is presented as the victim of an uncaring, demanding society that refuses to help or understand him. In fact, Johnny is the victimizer who chose his way of life. If Johnny's childhood was unfortunate and he did not have the love and guidance of caring parents, we can feel sad for Johnny, but does that mean we must accept his unacceptable behavior? Certainly not. Adult Johnny is responsible for all of the passengers on his bus. If Johnny is allowed to blame his parents, society, or his feelings for his behavior, society is accepting Johnny's worldview that *he*—not the person he plundered—is the victim. This upside-down perspective is central to Johnny's chaotic, narcissistic world of blurred boundaries, but it is anathema to the world of rational thought. If it is to be orderly, civilized society must demand personal accountability and objective reality rooted in the present. Judges and juries must enforce the laws of adulthood, regardless of the offender's childhood experience or state of mind.

December 4

Behavior is a Choice

AMERICANS shake their heads in wonder and cannot understand why rapists and murderers do what they do, yet are not made to pay the consequences for their choices. Behavior is a choice. Behavior stems from thought. If society wants to understand the criminal, we must be willing to investigate how the criminal thinks. The criminal has the same anthem as the narcissist: "I want what I want when I want it." Criminals are narcissists, but not every narcissist is a criminal. The difference between them is that one stays within the law and one does not. Both operate from a very underdeveloped psychological framework. In childhood, it is difficult to predict who will grow up to be a responsible citizen, who will remain underdeveloped and become a narcissistic adult, and who will become a career criminal. Each outcome is ultimately determined by the choices the individual makes. It is irrational to argue that poor Johnny did not have a responsible role model. That argument diminishes the choices and hard work of every other individual who was without loving parents and a gentle

childhood but who still managed to grow into responsible adulthood. Some of those children relied on a
teacher or older sibling or family friend to help them
grow up. After childhood, it is counterproductive to
blame anyone but *self*. Remember, there are different
standards of behavior for children because they are in
the learning process.

Children are society's true victims because they
are powerless and have no choices. Adults have
choices even if they do not see them. If a driver runs
a red light and goes to court arguing that he did not
see the light, it is the judge's job to point out that it
is the driver's responsibility to see traffic lights. That
is, adults must be held accountable for their behaviors. Period. No excuses. When Johnny was ten, he
was still considered to be "in process." At eighteen he
is entirely responsible for his behavior because as a
chronological adult he has choices even if he does not
see them. Period. No excuses. Johnny is responsible
for every passenger on his bus, including all of his
inner children. It is up to Johnny to control them. It
is up to Johnny to remain in control of his bus.

Part of the disintegration of civilized society is due
to the shift in behavior standards from the accountability demanded by the responsible adult to the
excuses that satisfy the child. To the degree that our
society accepts excuses rather than accountability,
we have accepted the norms of the narcissist rather
than the standards of responsible adulthood. When
society accepts Johnny's impoverished childhood as
an excuse for his stealing, or accepts Johnny's violent

childhood as an excuse for his violence, society has sanctioned the destructive behavior of Johnny's angry inner child. It has accepted the behavior of childhood in adulthood and has accepted the past as the present. If the responsible adult segment of our society ever totally relinquishes control to the narcissists, we will have utter chaos and a complete collapse of civilized life. The present will have totally surrendered to the governance of the past.

Margin Between Chronological Age and Psychological Development

THE margin between chronological age and psychological development is especially catastrophic when angry inner children organize themselves into gangs. If Johnny can assemble a group of like-minded, angry inner children, he has created a gang. Gangs are an example of what happens when society allows the angriest of inner children to get behind the wheel. Society needs to take a much stronger stand against the intrusion of gangs into civilized life. In the same way that a parent would pull a child out of the driver's seat of a car, so must we physically remove gangs from our midst. No excuses. Gangs develop in an environment that lacks effective adult supervision. Imagine the microcosm of a family with several young children. If the parents choose to absolve themselves of their adult responsibilities and permanently leave home, what will happen to the children? With no responsible adult intervention or guidance, the strongest personality among the children will emerge as the leader. It might be the oldest but not necessarily. Soon the pressures of survival will overcome the novelty of being unsupervised, and the excitement of being able to do whatever they want will surrender to fear. When this happens, there is often a change in leadership.

In William Golding's classic novel, *Lord of the Flies,* the author chronicles the sequential breakdown of civilized life as a group of stranded, completely unsupervised English schoolboys discard the rules that govern civilized behavior. Initially, a peaceful election is held, and Ralph, the voice of reason, secures the leadership role. Rules of order are established, and a system is implemented to organize the group and ensure their survival until help arrives. Ralph articulates the need to build and maintain a signal fire. A sense of fairness prevails. Soon, one of the younger boys announces that he has seen a "beastie." The group perceives their safety to be threatened, and an atmosphere of fear prevails. In this environment of fear, the group eventually abandons Ralph's civilized leadership and yields to the totalitarian governance of a new leader, Jack. In an atmosphere of fear, the boys regress to primitive states of mind where they can recognize the exercise of power as the only existence of power. Jack is recognized as their leader because he demonstrates the force of aggression. The young child, like the narcissist, is not psychologically developed enough to appreciate the power of restraint. The boys on the island see Jack as powerful and Ralph as weak. They feel safer with Jack and give him their loyalty. This is an extremely convoluted and dangerous environment psychologically. When aggression is seen as being more powerful than restraint, the most brutal leader is regarded as being the safest to follow.

This regressive state of mind explains the sometimes-baffling loyalty of members to their gangs, disciples to their cults, citizens to their totalitarian governments, and children to their abusive parents. Fear is an extremely powerful motivator for behavior because it has the capacity to catapult the individual back in time to a very primitive state of mind. Fear induces regression. When a frightened inner child is driving the bus, it is extremely difficult to separate him from his gang, cult, country, or abusive parent. Frightened inner children simply do not make rational, adult choices because they have not acquired the necessary thinking skills. A young child cannot survive independently; a young adult, however, can survive if her state of mind remains in adulthood. When a frightened inner child is in control, separateness is an issue in itself.

SEPARATION

SEPARATION is the experiencing of one's alone-ness. A chronological child's fear of separateness is rooted in reality because she cannot survive on her own. If she is separated, she will perish. The separation anxiety of the chronological child is adaptive. The separation anxiety of the chronological adult is maladaptive because an adult can survive on her own. When the chronological adult is frightened and her inner child takes command, she fears separation again because she is back in the world of her past where the fear originated. Her dread of aloneness derives from her childhood, where aloneness meant death. In this state of mind, the individual will do anything not to be alone. It is her survival response. Her fear engenders compliance. When her fright-ened inner child is driving the bus, her perceptual reality is that aloneness means death. The sequence is that fear engenders regression; regression engen-ders separation anxiety; separation anxiety engenders compliance. Any individual or group that seeks compliance can use fear as a tool to induce regression and compliance. A frightened child reasons that if she does what the aggressor wants, the aggressor will not hurt her. She strikes a deal. In the magical thinking of the child, she is convinced that this strategy will protect her. She remains hopeful that her compliance will shield her. She becomes a pleaser. The error in this thinking is that tyrants do not respect rules or deals. The despot will brutalize the child regardless of how compliant she becomes. The child is not psychologically developed enough to recognize the futility of her hopefulness. The boys on William Golding's island answer the broader societal question, "Why does a parent relinquish his power to his real child?" It is the parent's inner child that gives away the power. Just like the boys on the island, the parent's inner child is responding to his fear of aloneness with compliance. Bullies, regardless of age, can extort power from frightened inner children regardless of their chronological ages. Little Johnny can extort power from his parent with the same tools that any adult bully can manipulate his gang.

William Golding offers an insightful ending to *Lord of the Flies.* Jack, the symbol of chaos and destruction, is hunting Ralph, the symbol of civilized life. Ralph collapses on the beach in exhaustion and is rescued by a naval officer, the adult symbol of order. The irony is that the fire started by Jack to smoke Ralph out of hiding was what led the naval officer to the island. It was the signal fire that Ralph had insisted upon initially that saved him. In the end, the rational, adult state of mind prevails, but Golding's description of the intense struggle for power is very instructive. It vividly parallels the sequential breakdown of civilized life that ensues when a frightened inner child is in control of the bus.

Society's survival depends upon the psychological growth and development of its citizens. The fact that Ralph is rescued is optimistic, but the fact that a military officer does the rescuing is significant. Historically, whenever a social system breaks down in any society in the world, that society is vulnerable to takeover by military coup. The cycle of governance is that military rule immediately fills the leadership vacuum of chaos. Order is restored by dictatorship. Fascist rule, like gangs and abusive parents, employs fear to engender compliance. Fascist rule persists as long as the level of force and brutality it employs succeeds in keeping the frightened inner children of its citizens mobilized. If their rational, adult states of mind surface, these citizens will be able to organize resistance groups and oppose the fascists. Or, if another force capable of overthrowing the fascist regime intervenes, civilized leadership can replace the fascists. In either case, the ruling power does not relinquish its position without a struggle.

Social systems that promote growth are those that encourage freethinking and free choice. Families led by parents who have achieved rational, adult states of mind can offer their children environments conducive to growth. Political structures that encourage growth are those that offer their citizens a maximum of free expression and choices. Repressive totalitarian governments, gangs, and abusive families are not conducive to growth, and they are driven by fear. A liberal democracy is the system of government most conducive to rational, adult thought. Within the infrastructure of a liberal democracy, the rational adult has the power and responsibility to vote and establish or change existing structures. Dear America, it is time for the rational adult members of society to acknowledge Civil War II and redefine our priorities so that we can achieve a civilized way of life.

ACHIEVING A CIVILIZED SOCIETY

HOW do we achieve a civilized way of life? A civilized society requires its chronological adult citizens to be developed emotionally. It demands a public and private commitment to the growth process of its children. What facilitates growth? First, one must make a commitment to personal responsibility for one's behavior regardless of state of mind. This commitment must be made universally in society by individuals, parents, mental health professionals, government officials—all segments of society that have an interest in the survival of civilized life. Second, we need to make a commitment to living in objective reality. Being in objective reality requires a commitment to staying in the present, which includes the recognition that innocent children are the real victims because they have no choices and, therefore, no power. An adult victimizer is not a victim today—even if he was victimized as a child and is psychologically underdeveloped—because today he has choices.

He has reached age eighteen chronologically and is legally responsible for his actions. If a victimizer does not recognize that his angry inner child is driving his bus, he is personally responsible for acquiring this information. Ignorance is not a valid defense for unacceptable behavior. If emotionally he is underdeveloped and still perceives himself as a victim living in the environment of his childhood, then he is in need of education and therapy to help him develop a strong, rational, adult state of mind and a reality-based sense of time. He needs to pack his bags and leave the subjective, perceptual reality of his past and move into the objective reality of the present. Moving day is frightening but necessary.

TIME-WARPING

THE movement back and forth between objective reality and subjective reality is called time-warping. The time-warping that accompanies the state of mind of an inner child is extremely important to understand. It is parallel to the soldier who comes out of the jungle and does not know that the war is over. When he is back in America and hears a traffic helicopter overhead, he perceives himself to be under attack. He sees a truck on the road and perceives an enemy convoy. In his earlier environment of actual war, he really was being attacked. But now it is a perceptual war, not an actual war, and his warlike behavior is no longer appropriate. He needs to acquire a reality-based sense of time. He needs the civilian that he is, not the soldier that he was, to be driving his bus. Shall society empathize with this man? Certainly. Can society afford to let him take out his machine gun and fire away at passing motorists? Certainly not. Regardless of his sense of time or state of mind, he is still responsible for his behavior. If he does not have the skills to remain in the present and cannot discipline himself to act responsibly in society, he must be removed from society until he is in control of himself. It is not a punitive response for him to be removed; it is a survival response for society. It is parallel to removing a two-year-old from the driver's seat of a car. In reality, if a child gets behind the wheel, it is the responsible reaction to remove him. Likewise, when a chronological adult has a historic inner child behind the wheel speeding and ignoring traffic laws or signals, it is the responsible reaction for society to remove him.

Some argue that this standard of behavior is unfair, that it unjustly penalizes victims of war and victims of child abuse. Consider the alternative. If society permits the soldier to remain in his warring state of mind when there is no real war, it has allowed the soldier's unreal state of mind to create a real war in society. Eventually some motorist will shoot back. Civil War II is the clash between the present reality of the responsible adult and the past reality of the narcissist. The narcissist, like the time-warping soldier, lives in an unreal environment consistent with his unreal state of mind. Trauma has tethered each to the past. Mentally, the narcissist lives in the past in a place of infancy or early childhood where there are no rules or boundaries. His behavior is appropriate to that environment but not to civilized society. His past reality intrudes on the present reality. The soldier lives in a place of war. His behavior is appropriate to that environment but not to civilized society. It is the narcissist's responsibility to emerge from infancy, and it is the soldier's responsibility to emerge from the jungle. It is the adult's responsibility to acquire the self-discipline of psychological growth, and it is society's responsibility to remove him if he has not.

Growing up psychologically is what eventually empowers the child. Physically he can leave a hurtful environment when he is old enough to go, but it is his emotional growth that will free him. If the adolescent leaves physically but remains a child emotionally, he will still perceive himself as a victim, even in adulthood—no matter where he lives. He will remain emotionally tethered to the past and will reenact the patterns of his childhood. This is a critical issue because it underlies the regressive behavior of so many chronological adults. To be a survivor instead of a victim, one must grow up psychologically. Physical growth is not enough. A survival mentality demands the movement to an adult state of mind; a victim mentality remains in childhood. A survivor leaves; a victim stays.

PSYCHOLOGICAL DEVELOPMENT OF A SOCIETY

SOCIETY is composed of individuals whose psychological development determines the nature and quality of life in that society. To examine the psychological development of a society we must look at individual patterns of behavior established in childhood that are reenacted in adulthood. What does it mean to reenact the patterns of childhood? First, we must distinguish between behavioral patterns that are conscious and those that are unconscious. Since the learning process is rooted in mimicry, both behavioral patterns originate as imitations of role models or events. If the child lives with parents who argue and scream, he perceives arguing and screaming to be the norm. Only when he ventures outside his home does he have any basis for comparison. If his friends' parents also argue and scream, his perception of the norm is reinforced. If he encounters other parents who speak to each other with respect, the child has been exposed to a new behavior pattern and can see that not all parents act alike. He has established a basis for comparison. This presents the child with the information to make a conscious choice. Will he imitate the screamer or the courteous role model? Will he become rude or polite? Even if all the adults he sees are screamers, there is still the possibility that the child will choose civility by *imagining* the possibility. Fantasy is a very important part of childhood. It helps the child choose who he will become. Books, movies, and television programs augment fantasy. They can help the child decide who he wants to become in the absence of real-life, positive role models. The content of children's entertainment is extremely important because it offers fantasy role models. The child might read about gentle relationships or watch civilized relationships dramatized on television or at the movies. Books, films, and television programs that dramatize how life can be are not irrelevant, romanticizing drivel. To the contrary, they provide a powerful alternative to life as it is. Art that depicts life as it can be is an immensely constructive force in our society. If society recognizes the need for positive role models, it will also recognize the need for positive entertainment.

Behavior patterns range anywhere from benign to toxic. Since the learning process of childhood is rooted in mimicry, the quality of the behavior being imitated is a critical variable. Rudeness is not as desirable as courtesy, but clearly it is not as dangerous as abusiveness. In any case, one must always remember the contribution of the child to the adult she eventually becomes. Adults choose to be abusive or gentle parents; consciously or unconsciously they choose to repeat the way they were raised or choose to change those patterns. Some adults cling to the faulty idea that the violence in their childhoods was harmless. These are the mothers and fathers who proudly claim, "My parents beat me to teach me. They loved me. I turned out all right." These mothers and fathers cling to the fiction that love and violence belong together. To preserve the illusion that their parents' behavior was loving, they perpetuate the myth by repeating it with their own children. The repetition is a defensive behavior designed to keep the truth of their own childhoods hidden. The truth is that violence done to children is not love—it is violence. Behavior patterns, whether toxic or benign, begin in childhood and continue into adulthood unrestrained unless the individual takes responsibility for her life and consciously chooses to change them. A survivor leaves; a victim stays.

Unconscious behavior patterns differ from conscious patterns in that they are generally born of a particular trauma. Reenactments of trauma are unconscious repetitions of a specific painful event and/or responses to that event. Death, divorce, suicide, sexual abuse, emotional abuse, and physical abuse are all specific traumas that can result in these reenactments. The trauma may or may not be remembered, but the connection between the past trauma and the present behavior pattern is not made. Trauma freezes the individual in time. Whether the person is two years old, ten years old, or twenty years old, the trauma silences and shuts him down emotionally. He continues to grow physically, but his emotional growth is arrested. The reenactment occurs every time the shut-down inner child is mobilized to commandeer the steering wheel and drive the bus. The inner child is activated whenever the present conditions remind him of the past. Reenactments are unconscious. They are the hallmark of addictions. They are the silent, encoded language of the inner child speaking through behavior. Reenactments dramatize the unsafe situation of the inner child. The primary goal of the inner child is safety. He cannot feel safe until his situation is understood. Reenactments are triggered any time the traumatized inner child feels unsafe. Each time the frozen entity is in control of the person's mind, the reenactment proceeds. His reenactments represent his automatic response to danger, even though the response is no longer adaptive. He is physically living in the objective reality of the present but emotionally living in the subjective reality of the past. Past and present collide. His responses to the past cannot protect him in the present. He remains unsafe.

Reenactments of trauma are destructive to self and to others. Reenactments are unconscious responses to perceived danger by the traumatized inner child. Reenactments recur relentlessly until they are recognized and resolved. They are the inner child's personal silent movie played over and over and over again. Addictions are reenactments. Reenactments must be exposed, decoded, and confronted consciously in order to restart the growth process and free the individual from the past. The unconscious connection between past trauma and present behavior must be brought to consciousness so that it can be resolved. Trauma is the source of reenacting. The more toxic the behavior being reenacted the more dangerous the reenactment to the individual and to those around her. Reenactments stop only when the trauma is revealed and confronted. The connection between past trauma and present behavior is one of cause and effect; it is the connection between abuse and addiction. The traumatized inner child simply cannot stop trying to be heard until she is heard. She cannot be safe until she is heard and understood.

Dear America, we must listen. The prevalence of addiction in our country confirms the widespread trauma to children here. Addictions cannot be extinguished until we are willing to discover the traumas that cause them. Addictions ravage society externally and the individual internally. We will not be safe in society until our children are safe externally and our inner children are safe within ourselves, in our own minds.

ADDICTIONS

SOME addictions are more devastating than others. The level of destruction is directly proportional to the destructiveness of the behavior being reenacted. Consider adult Johnny's social pattern of breaking off romantic relationships as soon as they get serious. He recognizes this destructive pattern in himself but cannot seem to stop the inevitable termination of the relationship. Johnny is thirty years old. When he was seventeen, his father, once a successful businessman, lost his business and committed suicide.

Suicide is always traumatic for the family. In Johnny's case, he adored his father and felt devastated and abandoned after his death. Love and trust necessarily generate feelings of vulnerability. In his adulthood, whenever Johnny begins to have feelings of love and trust, his inner adolescent, who is frozen in time at the moment of his father's suicide, feels unsafe and is mobilized. The adolescent senses danger and attempts to protect the self. The reenactment begins. Johnny's adolescent inner child is driving the bus. Johnny does to his girlfriend what his father did to him. He abandons her. Johnny does not realize that his girlfriend's feelings of trust, love, and vulnerability parallel Johnny's own adolescent feelings toward his father. When he breaks up with her, he abandons her suddenly the way his father abandoned him. It is necessary for Johnny to know that the girlfriend loves him or else the terms of the reenactment are not met. He must wait until she loves him and then suddenly break up with her. The problem for Johnny is that he cannot enjoy a long-term, loving relationship. The problem for the girlfriend is that she is destined to be rejected unless Johnny exposes and resolves his reenactment. None of this has anything to do with her. It is not personal. She has just bumped into Johnny's trauma; she has unknowingly stepped into his silent movie. Johnny does not realize that breaking up with his girlfriend is his inner child's attempt to keep him safe from the feelings of loss associated with his father's suicide. His past has intruded on his present. Johnny feels compelled to repeat the sequence of his past. He is an addict.

When society romanticizes Johnny's macho "love them and leave them" behavior, or hails him as a "born" bachelor, it reinforces a reenactment. It helps Johnny embrace his addiction rather than expose his reenactment. Often, people who reenact have an awareness of their destructive, repetitive behavior patterns, but more often than not they have no idea that they are reenacting childhood traumas. They come to believe that it is their nature, and they simply do not make the connection that a past trauma is compelling the current behavior. Whether or not the trauma is remembered, the connection is unacknowledged and the behavior continues.

The hallmark of a reenactment is that it persists relentlessly unless there is effective intervention to dismantle it. Any attempt at dismantling that does not address the trauma at the base of the addiction is entirely futile. The trauma and the feelings associated with the trauma must be recognized, felt, and resolved. Remedies that address the symptoms of addiction, not the cause, are useless. Attempts to identify an "addictive" personality overlook the core trauma. Identifying an "addictive" personality only illustrates that if the inner child is not heard in one form, he will choose another until he is heard.

Genetic explanations for addiction are entirely misguided. The fact that addictive behavior is so resistant to change is not an issue of heredity; it is testimonial to the fact that the underlying cause of addiction remains hidden. The remedy for a reenactment is to expose the past trauma and to reveal how the trauma is being reenacted in the present. It is the connection between past and present that is critical.

Often people can acknowledge the trauma and can recognize the patterns in their behaviors, but unless the connection between the two is revealed the behaviors persist. When the connection is manifest and the reenactment exposed, the rational adult can again take command of the bus. Only if Johnny understands the connection between his father's suicide and his own social pattern can he change the pattern.

Otherwise, he slavishly repeats the pattern with each new partner, never understanding what motivates him to act this way. When Johnny recognizes the connection, he will be able to hear the pain of the adolescent, but he will not relinquish control of his adult mind to him. Only when the inner child is finally heard can he feel safe. Once the inner child is safe he quiets down, and the rational adult can enjoy an adult relationship without his inner child interrupting it. The quality of Johnny's life is improved. He lives in the present. He is no longer an addict.

DIVORCE

NOT all reenactments are as dramatic as Johnny's. Not all traumas are as dramatic as suicide. What about divorce? Much attention has been paid to the young children of divorced parents. How will living alternately with one parent and then the other affect them? How do issues of loyalty affect the children? What happens if the custodial parent decides to remarry? What are the complications of blended families? These questions address issues relevant to children living at home. What about the millions of young adults who are children of the divorced couples in our country who are now living away from home trying to establish adult relationships of their own? How does the trauma of their parents' divorce affect their adult lives? Will they necessarily reenact the trauma?

Let us begin with their expectations—the legacy of their parents' divorce. Often the expectation of children of divorce is that they will be abandoned. Permanence and consistency are not reality for them, and the collapse of their family structure has threatened their safety. Children of divorce live in a state of perpetual uncertainty. What will happen to me? Where will I live? Who will take care of me? Will they stop loving me, too? Who can I trust? Who can I believe? What is real? The trauma of divorce extends into the next generation's ability to trust and believe that lasting, committed relationships are possible. The alarming frequency of divorce validates the fear that nothing lasts forever.

It is the long-term effects of divorce that society needs to address, not just the short-term needs of the children living at home during the divorce. If the children of divorce reenact their childhoods, they will relive the trauma of their past with current spouses and end up divorced themselves. They will be addicts—individuals unconsciously compelled to re-create and repeat the patterns of their childhoods.

DECEMBER 12

INVULNERABLE CHILDREN

THE vast majority of children who are emotionally, physically, and sexually abused will also
unconsciously re-create with extraordinary exactness
the events of their childhoods. The exceptions are
the children who manage to reverse their childhood
experiences rather than reenact them. These particular children respond to trauma differently than most
victims. They do not perceive themselves as helpless victims. To the contrary, they see themselves as
survivors with a future. They have hope. Rather than
unconsciously repeating their childhood experiences
in adulthood, they consciously choose to change the
destructive patterns of their childhoods. They are
builders who reject destruction and choose constructive lives. They have a plan. It is not their good
intentions that separate the exceptions from the rule;
it is the implementation of the plan that is extraordinary. These invulnerable children manage to be
constructive and, against all odds, do not reenact the
destructive experiences of their childhoods.

Unfortunately, reenactments usually come in the

form of destruction of self or destruction of others. Addictions are self-destructive reenactments. Rape, torture, and murder are examples of destruction to others. No child is born destructive; it is a learned behavior. No child is born violent; it is the violence done to children that creates violent children. The increasing number of children who kill is an alarming trend. Society is shocked, appalled, and confused by a child killing another child. Killing is the most devastating reenactment. When a child kills, he is reenacting the position of both victim and victimizer; in this drama, he combines the brutality of the victimizer with the revenge of the victim. It is complete destruction. Like any other violent criminal, trauma has halted the psychological growth process of the child who kills.

Social theories that explain violence in terms of television and movies are superficial explanations that have the sequence reversed. Media does not create violent children. It is the violence done to children that creates the market for violence in the entertainment media, both from the producing and the consuming points of view. Sometimes the seeds of destructiveness bloom early, and a child who kills is the result. Sometimes the seeds of destructiveness take decades to bloom. They take root in childhood and don't fully ripen until adolescence or adulthood. It is this time lapse that often obscures the cause-and-effect connection between early childhood abuse and the appearance of symptoms later in life. Even the existence of symptomatic behavior is difficult to identify in later life when reenactments are cloaked by genetic explanations for behavior.

If we accept alcoholism, drug addiction, food addiction, and addiction to violence as genetically determined behaviors, we lose the opportunity to expose these reenactments and cannot heal from the initiating trauma. The most difficult causal connection to establish occurs when the childhood abuse has been completely repressed. The repression that is adaptive for survival in childhood is maladaptive when it is advanced into adulthood because it conceals the causal connection between abuse and destructive behavior. The remedy for reenactments is always the same. The driving psychological connections between the person's childhood trauma and her adult behavior must be exposed. The trauma must be recognized, and the associated feelings must be felt. The inner child must be able to speak and be heard to feel safe. The inner child's experience and pain must be acknowledged by the adult she has become. As long as the chronological adult denies and camouflages her childhood trauma with addiction, the reenactment will continue. Past and present must be distinguished so that the inner child feels safe within the adult she has become.

The child of divorce has much in common with the child of abuse, the child of suicide, and the time-warping soldier. Each has been traumatized and shut down emotionally. Each unconsciously relives the trauma of the past in the present and is unaware of the motivating connections between them. Each feels unsafe and blurs the boundaries of time and space when the frightened inner child takes over and drives the bus. Each addiction or instance of violence to others is a reenactment of the person's own unresolved childhood trauma. Every reenactment is acted out in the nonverbal language of the inner child. Understanding the encoded language of the inner child is the adult's responsibility to himself. To be in touch with one's real history is to free oneself from the relentless repetition of the past. To acknowledge and feel the fear, sadness, pain, and powerlessness of the inner child is to finally hear and validate that child's life experience. Consciousness has been restored. Only then can the growth process proceed and the healing process succeed.

CAUSAL CONNECTION BETWEEN CHILDHOOD TRAUMA AND ADULT DESTRUCTIVENESS

WHY is exposing the causal connection between childhood trauma and adult destructiveness resisted so vehemently? Why do reenactments persist so relentlessly? The answer is to be found in the state of mind of the frightened inner child. The frightened inner child fights desperately to avoid reexperiencing the excruciating pain of her childhood. Fear is the tyrannizing force that motivates her, and safety is her absolute priority. The frightened inner child knows why she is afraid even if the adult she has become has no idea. The inner child does not understand concepts of space and time. She is certain that her subjective reality is objective reality. The threat is real to her. The reality of the inner child parallels the reality of the dreamer. In the dream state, the inner child's state of mind prevails. When the dreamer awakes, the adult state of mind regains control. When an inner child is driving the bus during waking hours, it is parallel to a dreamer making decisions about reality.

The frightened inner child resists all efforts to revisit his trauma because he perceives revisiting as reexperiencing. The struggle between the perceptual realities of the inner child and the adult can be resolved only if the inner child feels safe enough to tell his story to the adult he has become. The adult must listen. Only then will the adult understand the encoded language of his reenactments and be able to reassure his inner child that the threat to the child's safety no longer exists. His childhood is over. He is safe now. The adult he has become will protect the inner child. The chronological adult must develop the emotional infrastructure of adulthood to protect his own inner child. He must remain in an adult state of mind where reason, not fear, governs his behavior.

Growing up psychologically is a challenge and a choice. It demands a commitment to objective reality and the awareness that childhood shapes adulthood. Growing up psychologically requires mindfulness and a commitment to living in the present. It recognizes that the past can hurt us only if we refuse to confront it and thereby remain tethered to it.

The genetic explanation for behavior obstructs psychological growth because it denies the causal connection between abuse and addiction. The heredity defense is anathema to healing because it camouflages child abuse in genetics. That is, the addict is seen as a product of his genes rather than a victim of child abuse. Well-meaning researchers, psychologists, and social workers unintentionally help perpetuate child abuse when they advocate genetics instead of trauma as the base of addiction. We must expose the abuse of children in order to end it, and that means exposing the connection between abuse and addictive behavior. Only the courage to confront the events of the past will free the addict. She needs the support of an enlightened society and a mental health community to help her. She needs to be safe. Psychological growth needs to be the individual's choice and society's choice if we are to live in a safe, rational society of responsible adults, rather than a dangerous, chaotic world run by frightened inner children.

Choosing a Survival Mentality

IF we allow the chronological adult, driven by her frightened inner child, to remain unrestrained in society with her reenactments unexposed, we have chosen to be her victim. We have collaborated with the victimizer to be her victim. It is a choice for responsible citizens to tolerate the irresponsibility of others or to demand responsibility. If we choose to remain a society of victims, we are culpable. We have victimized ourselves and sentenced ourselves to death because we have given up our power and our tools to survive. What shall we do? Where shall we begin? How do we choose life and a survival mentality?

If we choose life and a survival mentality, then we need to begin by reinforcing society's most potent infrastructure: the family. If we choose life and a survival mentality, then we must begin with a safe family. Safety is a human right. Every child is entitled to be safe physically, emotionally, and sexually. Children simply are not property. Society has begun this journey to safety by acknowledging that wives are not their husband's property; human beings belong to themselves. Domestic violence against women is now a crime. The next step toward a safe society is acknowledging that children belong to themselves. Violence against children is criminal and must be treated as a crime. What is criminal behavior against a stranger must be deemed criminal against a child. This shift redefines what is and is not acceptable parenting behavior. Thought precedes behavior. The shift from thinking of children as property to thinking of children as human beings is the basis of child safety. If we are ever going to have a safe America, we must make child safety at home a priority.

The job of responsible parenting is in need of serious support by every institution in society. Parenting classes should be a mandatory part of any educational curriculum offered in junior and senior high schools. There must be no confusion regarding what the "good" parent should try to accomplish. We must explicitly define the appropriate role, responsibilities, and goals of parenthood. The parent's role is to guide the child to adulthood. The parent's responsibilities are to provide safety, nurturing, consistency, and love. Self-sufficiency and responsible adulthood must be clearly defined as the goals toward which all education strives. Elementary education should introduce to the young child the role, responsibilities, and goals of childhood. The role of the child is to be a student of life. His responsibilities are to learn and to become increasingly responsible for his behavior. The goal of childhood is to emerge from narcissism and become a self-sufficient, responsible adult.

Whether Jenny becomes a tradeswoman, a teacher, a doctor, or a factory worker, the foundation for civilized life demands that she not remain a snatcher. If Jenny chooses to become a mother, she needs to be a responsible role model. Jenny cannot give what she does not have. If her parents were not responsible and she did not learn responsibility elsewhere, growth oriented psychotherapy is Jenny's next line of defense against permanent narcissism. Psychotherapy must be destigmatized so that psychological services can be perceived as in-depth teaching. The goal of treatment is to provide a safe environment where the inner child is free to tell her story. As the individual listens, she begins to know herself and understand her childhood experience; that is, she becomes acquainted with the passengers on her bus and each life's experience. She can hear and see the child she once was at different stages of life. Successful psychotherapy uncovers the forgotten events and feelings from the past, particularly the trauma that shut the child down psychologically. The therapeutic process restarts the psychological growth process. The individual begins to grow up psychologically and develop a rational, adult state of mind capable of nurturing the inner child she once was. The psychologically mature, rational adult can identify and hear her inner children but demands that her rational adult make the decisions. The rational adult, not one of her inner children, drives her bus. Psychotherapy is just out-of-sequence growing up. As long as the therapist is a sensitive, rational adult committed to the goals of self-sufficiency and responsible adulthood, psychotherapy is an extremely effective educational alternative. A therapist, like a parent, cannot be effective if an inner child is driving his bus.

It is helpful to remember that it does not matter where we start out in life; it matters where we finish. We all start out as narcissistic babies. The goal is to finish the growth process as rational, self-sufficient adults. Sooner is better than later, but later is better than never.

Even when an individual successfully attains responsible adulthood, his inner battle continues because achieving a rational, adult state of mind is only the first half of the maturation process. Maintaining a state of responsible adulthood is an ongoing challenge. The inner children on the bus are constantly competing with the adults on the bus for control. The pressures of daily life, the provocation of real-life children, and the inevitable crises of life cycles threaten to destabilize the responsible adult. He longs to return to a time of life when he enjoyed the comforts of dependency and did not have to worry about household bills, mortgage payments, or college expenses. He yearns for a moment of relief. At this time, the responsible adult's rational state of mind is vulnerable to a psychological coup. The narcissistic inner child fights for the driver's seat. If the responsible adult wrests the steering wheel from him, the adult regains his power, stabilizes himself, and can decide to return to the adult world of work and commitments. If the narcissistic child has managed to hijack the bus, he might walk out on his wife and family, have an extra-marital affair, quit his job, beat his children, or any number of other irresponsible choices—all because his irrational, narcissistic inner child is making the decisions.

Over and over again, men and women make irresponsible choices that are impulsive and damaging to them. The hallmark of their inner struggles is that the people are at a loss to explain how they could have behaved in such a manner. They are sorry, and they want another chance. Another chance for what?

Again, the fundamental question must be asked to explain unexplainable behavior: "Who's driving the bus?" If an individual seeks relief from the demands of his life and an inner child is driving his bus, he just walks away from his problems. This response is predictable for a young child. It becomes confusing when a chronological adult walks away and then expects another chance to do better, just as the young child would. So, "another chance" is a reference to the adult state of mind that is asking for another chance to remain a responsible adult. In this example, it is up to his wife to decide whether or not she wants to grant him this opportunity. The issue here is complex. Both husband and wife have choices. The husband can choose to retain the narcissistic position and demand that the wife accept his regressive, unacceptable behavior. Or he can recognize that his inner child was driving his bus and ask his wife to understand this dynamic and stay with him while he strives to grow and learn to keep his adult in control of his bus. The wife must choose whether or not to trust him.

If he chooses growth, he is either sincere or insincere. If he is insincere, he is placating his wife; his choice is a manipulation of the narcissist, and his behavior will repeat itself. The next time he is under stress, he will behave irresponsibly again. If he is sincere, he is making a genuine commitment to the growth process of behavior change. If he has difficulty making the change or recognizing his narcissism, he can see a qualified therapist for help. Time will expose the nature of his choice. Behavior change, not promises of change, is the proof.

A child confuses thinking and doing; a rational adult does not. Will the husband's wife accept promises as if they are real change, or will she wait and see how he behaves? If promises satisfy her, then her inner child is driving her bus and this couple will stay stuck in a repetitive cycle of hurtfulness and forgiveness. When both partners have inner children driving their buses, they remain in a perpetual state of dysfunction. The prevalence of dysfunctional marriages in America today is evidence that many individuals choose narcissism as a way of life. If one partner grows up and develops into a rational adult, that partner will either leave the marriage or demand that the spouse also grow to preserve the marriage. The prevalence of divorce in America is evidence of the internal and external struggle for control within marriages. Being narcissistic and walking away from responsibilities is not the same thing as growing up and leaving a destructive marriage. Divorce is sometimes driven by the inner child reenacting a past trauma and is sometimes driven by the rational adult. Evidence that inner children are at the wheel in our society is pervasive in both the private sector and the public sector.

PSYCHOLOGICAL GROWTH

PSYCHOLOGICAL growth is a process that begins with the narcissism of infancy and, ideally, culminates in rational adulthood. Psychological growth needs to be our national priority. It is the rational, adult state of mind that is required for responsible decision-making in our lives. As adults we each have within us the inner children of our childhood and a rational adult who is struggling to take power away from our inner children. Civil War II begins internally, each within ourselves. The degree to which the rational adult prevails is the measure of one's mental health at any given moment. The ideal sequence of development is that a person begins as a narcissistic infant who is gently encouraged to relinquish her narcissism as she moves through childhood and adolescence. She learns to become a responsible adult. The necessary information is transferred through the exemplary behavior of responsible adult role models whom she admires and seeks to emulate.

As the person grows and gains more freedom and responsibility, she gives up her demand for unconditional love and acceptance and feels empowered by the control over her own life that she begins to possess. She now feels the power of self-confidence and the certainty that comes with knowing that she is in control of herself and can manage her own inner life. Her most developed, rational, adult state of mind is driving her bus, and she feels the strength of self-esteem. She has prevailed in her inner struggle to emerge from her original state of narcissism. She lives in the present moment. She feels her power and can sustain a rational, adult state of mind, even when pressured to regress. She can delay gratification; she can wait. She is productive in the workplace and feels useful. She enjoys the wonderment that committed, romantic relationships can provide. She has internalized her lessons and can be an effective, loving parent with her children. She is committed to the growth process. She is self-disciplined. She is at peace within and in harmony with her surroundings. Her rational, adult state of mind remains in control.

The reality of our nation, however, is far from this ideal. People sense that things are out of control. They know that something is wrong. They feel threatened and unsafe but cannot seem to identify the problem. Religious fundamentalists claim that the problem is a lack of prayer at home and in school. Politicians claim that it is "outside" influences that bring rampant crime and illegal drugs into our neighborhoods. They tell us that we need more jails. Sociologists and psychologists tell us that we are a society of helpless victims who cannot be blamed for our behavior. It is "mother's" fault or "father's" fault or the "system's" fault.

Reality shows us that we are at war with ourselves. Civil War II is an ongoing, psychological battle fought internally within self and externally between self and other over which state of mind will be in control. The healthy, progressive part of us strives to develop a rational, adult state of mind. The unhealthy, regressive part of us is compelled to return to the past where we are addicted to reenacting the unresolved events of our childhoods.

Civil War II is in evidence in all areas of American life, public and private. The casualties of the war are innumerable. Particularly painful are the addictions that derive from a lost struggle to the regressive demands of our inner children. Addictions defy space and time. They take us back to our past where they originate, they drive our present behavior, and they threaten to persist into the future unless exposed as reenactments. Families torn apart, lack of productivity in the workplace, abusive homes, and unsafe neighborhoods are all evidence of the disintegration of civilized life that accompanies a lost inner struggle to an angry and frightened inner child. The current state of our nation is a reflection of this lost war between the states of our minds. Why is this war so difficult for the rational, adult state of mind to win?

What makes it so difficult to develop and maintain a rational, adult state of mind? Why is it so difficult for some children to grow up? Why do some adults insist on remaining eternal children? Who becomes a rational adult, and who remains a narcissist? What are the obstacles to growth, and how can we remove them? If we remember that the task of childhood is to grow into responsible adulthood, we must first review what adulthood is and how it is successfully achieved.

Responsible adulthood is the state of mind attained by the person who has mastered the transition from childhood to adulthood. The responsible adult is a rational adult who is influenced by the emotions and experiences of his inner children, yet makes decisions based on the logical thinking of his reasoning mind. He lives in the present and is able to respond to the stimuli of his environment with restraint. He is in control of himself. The responsible adult has integrated the emotions of his inner children with the rational thought of his developed mind. He is a physical and emotional grownup living in present-day reality; his chronological and psychological ages are in equilibrium. Ideally, a child is drawn out of his initial state of total narcissism by the gentle love and nurturing of his parents, who provide strong male and female role models for him to emulate. The parents teach the child responsible behavior by behaving responsibly themselves. The ideal parents have a strong marriage and provide the child with the foundation for loyalty, commitment, and the ability to see another person's point of view. The parents treat each other and the children with respect and dignity. Each parent has a developed, rational, adult state of mind and is in control of each of his or her

own inner children. Each parent has defined boundaries, respects the boundaries and privacy of others,
and is committed to the principle that an individual
is entitled to live his own life. We teach our children
but do not own them. We guide our children to self-
sufficiency and productivity but cannot guarantee
their outcome because children have choices. In our
less-than-ideal world, we know that this combination
of positives is rare.

OBSTACLES TO PSYCHOLOGICAL GROWTH

THERE are three main obstacles to psychological growth that disrupt the learning process. All emanate from childhood and involve the parent-child, child-parent interaction. All involve the power struggle between states of mind within self and the states of mind between self and other. The first obstacle to psychological growth is incompetent parenting. Since it is impossible to give what you do not have or teach what you do not know, benign, incompetent parenting thwarts many childhoods. That is, the parent is well intentioned but has not developed a strong, rational, adult state of mind that can serve as a consistent, responsible role model to the child.

The incompetent parent cannot withstand the child's narcissistic challenge to her authority and ultimately surrenders to the child's narcissistic demand to remain a baby. The incompetent parent is ineffective because she does not have the inner strength to insist on the child's emergence from the state of narcissism. In this category are the well-meaning couples who come to parenting with very good intentions but very little understanding of what appropriate parenting involves. Often these couples believe that if they just give little Johnny what they lacked in their own childhoods, everything will be fine. The problem is immediately one of identification. Little Johnny's life belongs to little Johnny. The parents need to understand that they cannot remedy their own childhoods by anything they do with Johnny. Johnny's life is separate from their lives. Experience is a very powerful teacher. If the parents have learned from their own experiences, they can apply what they have learned but must never confuse their own lives with Johnny's life. If, for example, Johnny's father comes from a family where his own father was very stingy and controlling, Johnny's father might commit himself to a parenting style of generosity and flexibility. So far, Johnny's father is doing fine. If, however, he is so determined not to repeat Grandpa's mistakes that he becomes overindulgent and permissive, then his own childhood will have interfered with his effectiveness as a parent, and both father and son will suffer. Little Johnny will not have the firm guidance he needs to draw himself out of his narcissism, and Johnny's father will not understand why his son does not appreciate what the father works so hard to provide.

Well-intentioned parents consistently make the classic mistake of giving the child what they needed themselves, not what the child needs. When Johnny's father tries to right the wrongs of his own childhood through his son, he makes the mistake of confusing his own life with that of his son's. The father blurs the boundaries between his own childhood and Johnny's. To be an effective parent, it is essential to remember that we each have only one life to live: our own. We can never go back to rewrite the history of our own childhoods through our children. We can learn from our past experiences and try not to repeat the mistakes of our own parents, but we can never remedy our own impoverished childhoods through the lives of our children. We can only seek to enrich our children's lives by being effective parents. By helping our children emerge from their states of narcissism, we have done our jobs and can at least enjoy the parent part of the parent-child relationship. To heal the wounds of our own childhoods, we must nurture our inner children—a completely separate task from nurturing our outer children. An effective parent separates the two. An effective parent does not give her outer child what her own inner child needs.

Also in the category of ineffective parents are those doting parents who unwittingly give their peerless child inappropriate power and importance in the family. The sun rises and sets on the little darling's head. In this circumstance, if the parents recognize their mistake and try to reclaim their authority or simply have another child, an enormous power struggle ensues between parent and child. The child does not relinquish the crown without a fight. Incompetent parents are unable to help their children emerge from narcissism. The child of incompetent parents remains self-absorbed and underdeveloped unless he chooses to complete his growth process later in life. The remedies for incompetent parenting are classes designed to define the appropriate roles, responsibilities, and goals of the effective parent, and therapeutic sessions to help develop and strengthen the parents' responsible, adult states of mind.

The second obstacle to psychological growth is abusive parenting. In abusive circumstances, the child's biological clock keeps ticking, but his psychological clock is stopped by trauma. Emotional, physical, and sexual abuse of children in this country is rampant. It is the most serious threat to our nation's well-being. Abusive parenting is always the responsibility of the parent, even if that parent was abused as a child. Whoever is in a position of authority over the child has the choice to nurture or abuse that child. In our society, parents, stepparents, grandparents, baby-sitters, aunts, uncles, sisters, brothers, day-care workers, teachers, coaches, and strangers perpetrate the abuse of children. It is very serious and damaging to assume that an abused child was necessarily abused by the parent. The critical issue here is that the person with authority over the child, his caretaker, has a choice. When that person chooses to abuse, the child is always the victim. It is never the child's fault, even though the perpetrator tries to blame him. Any emotional or physical damage done to the child is the adult's fault, even if that adult was emotionally and physically abused as a child. Any sexual contact between adult and child is the adult's fault, even if that adult was sexually abused as a child. Repetition is not a valid defense for abuse.

The critical issue in defining obstacles to psychological growth is to clarify that the chronological adult with authority over the child is absolutely responsible for her own behavior, regardless of her personal history. Repetition is not inevitable. Not all abused children become abusive adults. However, there are so many who do that if society does not demand complete responsibility from perpetrators, then a generational cycle of abuse and repetition of abuse becomes the inevitable outcome. If our well-meaning social scientists and public officials continue to excuse inexcusable behavior because the abuser was abused in her own childhood, then we will sanction a generation of abusive adults living in the time warp of their own abusive childhoods. We will have a population of abusive parents reenacting their own childhood abuse in a perceptual reality of victimization. In this circumstance, the abusive parent is reenacting the brutal experience of her own inner child with her outer child. Again, the parent is confusing the boundary between herself and her child, but instead of giving the outer child what the inner child needs, she is giving the outer child what the inner child got. The incompetent parent and the abusive parent make the same fundamental mistake of time-warping back to their own childhoods. To avoid this calamity, it is essential that parents stay in the present time zone. They cannot let their inner children, who live in the past, dominate them because then their past determines their present decisions. Whether the parent tries to remedy his past or repeat it, he is still making the grievous error of living in the past. The present is where we need to be. Moving day is frightening but necessary.

The soldier who comes out of the jungle and does not know the war is over will make serious mistakes in judgment. Whether he chooses to wear civilian clothes or remain in uniform, he will still think like a soldier. Since behavior derives from thought, he will necessarily act like a soldier. If he misinterprets the sounds of a weather helicopter or the look of a truck and perceives himself to be under attack, he will "return" fire and shoot innocent civilians. The soldier is living in a perceptual war zone. His past has collided with his present. Like the soldier, there are a multitude of frightened, angry, abused Americans whose pasts have collided with the present. The abused child lives under siege in a warring environment where he is defenseless, emotionally and physically. If he survives physically and becomes a chronological adult, he may remain psychologically in the warring environment of his childhood. In this circumstance, the individual lives in the virtual reality of his perceptual war but is now old enough to arm himself.

Rapists, murderers, and child abusers are criminals. They are no longer abused children. They are chronological adults who have become abusive adults. The collision of objective reality and the adult's subjective reality creates an explosive atmosphere where innocent people are being victimized. It is critical in a civilized society that we live in objective reality where time and space are the here and now. Not being in touch with the reality of the moment, the basis of the insanity plea must be disallowed for the abusive adult as well as for the time-warping soldier.

A person is considered legally insane if, as a result of mental illness or mental retardation, she lacks substantial capacity to appreciate the wrongfulness of her conduct or to conform her conduct to the requirements of the law. In reality, the insane person is not just insane for the duration of her crime, but before and after it. The flaw in the insanity defense is that the legal description of insanity allows for "temporary" insanity. Any time an angry inner child is driving the bus, the individual is not in touch with the reality of the moment because she has time-warped back to the past. Can a child appreciate the wrongfulness of her conduct? Can a child conform her conduct to the requirements of the law? The loophole in the legal criteria defining insanity is that chronological adults are being excused as if they are children not responsible for their states of mind. A state of mind is fluid. At any time, a chronological adult can regress backward on his time line and function as an out-of-control child. Is he temporarily insane? Perhaps. Is he responsible for his state of mind? Absolutely. An individual's state of mind can explain his behavior but must never be allowed to excuse his behavior. Temporary insanity must be eliminated as a criminal defense in America.

The time-warping soldier, like the criminal,

must be disarmed and removed from society, and so must the abusive parent be disarmed and removed from the family, until each is equipped to live in the present. Each needs to develop psychologically. It is in society's self-interest to help these people grow up. Since we cannot go back in time and give that individual an ideal childhood, we can either tolerate his antisocial behavior or demand responsible behavior and help him build a new life. The task for him is to accept that abusive behavior will not be tolerated. He must be removed from society permanently or temporarily, depending on whether he chooses to grow up psychologically and live in the present or continue his irresponsible, destructive reenactments of the past. If he chooses growth, he will need help. It will be necessary for him to restart the learning process at the point where trauma stopped his psychological clock. A treatment program that provides a safe environment for him to recover from his own trauma is the civilized approach to healing. In a safe setting, he will be free to understand the effects of the abuse so that he can confront them and heal.

Denying abuse, accepting abuse, excusing abuse, or ignoring abuse only promotes more abuse. The only way to stop abuse is to confront it. The hallmark of an individual's rational, adult state of mind is that he stays in objective reality and lives in the present. He controls the inner children of his past and can nurture the outer children of his present. In this state of mind, he has the capacity to love and work— both necessary ingredients for civilized society. When he has achieved responsible adulthood, society can welcome him back.

The third obstacle to psychological growth is the least apparent. It is the child's own input into his growth process. Parents consistently overestimate their power. Even though they are the most powerful influence in the child's life, they are not the only influence. Parents mistakenly believe that they can guarantee the outcome of their parenting. The thought process of the well- intentioned parent is that raising a child is like baking bread; if you just follow the recipe, the dough will necessarily rise and turn into a wonderful loaf of bread. The flaw in this thinking is that children are not lumps of dough. These parents overlook the input of the child into the child's growth process. As the responsible adult attempts to help the child emerge from narcissism, the child is presented with choices. Jenny is told that it is not acceptable to snatch toys. Jenny has choices. Her responses to these choices are Jenny's input into her own growth process. She can cooperate and give back the toy gracefully, she can whine and moan about the unfairness of life and hand back the toy, or she can resist all efforts at civilizing her behavior, throw a temper tantrum, and refuse to give up the toy. The level of her resistance to growth indicates her level of attachment to her narcissistic way of life. Some kids grow up gracefully, some kids grow up kicking and screaming, and some kids never grow up at all. As Jenny gets older her contribution to her adult outcome increases dramatically. In later childhood and early adolescence, she can see differences in behavior among her peers and among the adults with whom she interacts. Jenny has more choices. If she doesn't like the way her parents behave, she can choose to behave like someone else's parent, an admired teacher, or a relative. She can emulate nurturing parents on television, in books, or at the movies. In her imagination, she can design the woman she wants to become and the life she wants to lead.

In childhood, the level of the child's dependency needs interact with the level of his parents' psychological development, but the outcome is ultimately determined by the choices Johnny makes as an adolescent and adult. If Johnny chooses babydom, he will remain in a state of perpetual narcissism; if Johnny chooses adulthood, he will complete the work of developing his rational, adult state of mind and become a productive member of society. Whether Johnny has ideal parents, incompetent parents, or abusive parents, Johnny's life belongs to Johnny. His adult outcome is a choice, and that choice is Johnny's.

If Johnny chooses narcissism as his way of life, he has a myriad of choices available to express his babydom. If Johnny experienced benign, incompetent parenting, he will probably be self-absorbed and inconsiderate but not toxic in his treatment of others. Perhaps he will have difficulty maintaining a serious relationship. He might find the early pursuit phase of a relationship exciting but will probably flee at the first gesture of obligation; any responsibility to another person will strike Johnny as an unacceptable restriction upon his personal freedom. True to his narcissistic perspective, Johnny will insist upon unconditional acceptance and approval. He will expect the commitment of his partner without any reciprocal obligation on his part. In the same way that little Johnny expected unconditional acceptance from his mother, adult Johnny expects unconditional acceptance from his partner. The double standard inherent in the narcissist's perspective derives from his childish perspective that is free of the constraints of adult reciprocity. The problem with adult Johnny's expectation is that it is no longer age appropriate. His functioning is acceptable for a two-year-old but not a twenty-year-old.

If adult Johnny partially develops psychologically, he might be able to make a commitment to another human being. He will probably find a woman who will baby him and take care of him, a woman who will applaud him for just existing and make no serious demands on him—in general, a woman who will treat him like his adoring mother did when he was fifteen. In this circumstance, Johnny is functioning at an adolescent level in which he can understand the adult principle of reciprocity but is not fully developed enough to deliver it on a regular basis. In general, Johnny will need to be the center of his wife's world and will not experience really serious conflict until his children are born. At that time, it is fairly predictable that Johnny will run into trouble. The jealousy that characterizes his narcissism will conflict with his ability to be a nurturing father. The demanding infant is soothed and comforted with food and caresses; the demanding adult expects the same treatment. In fact, in many cases it is the adult's envy of the handling of an infant that provokes serious problems within marriages. The father envies the wife's attentiveness to the baby (or vice versa), and a triangle of jealousy is established. The envious inner child of the father, the real child, and the wife are engaged in a power struggle. The inner child of the father has interfered with the upbringing of his real infant, and it has interfered in his marriage. Many divorces are the result of the narcissistic inner child of one of the spouses being in jealous conflict with a real child in the house. The father experiences the conflict of wanting to love his baby and being jealous of him. When his rational adult is in charge, the father can be loving and nurturing; he can enjoy the baby and share in the child's care with his wife. When his envious inner child takes over, he resents the child and will end up in conflict with his wife over the baby. And so his psychological war continues.

The necessity of growing up psychologically and freeing oneself from the bondage of demanding inner children is evident. Parents who remain slaves to their inner children live lives of anguish and suffering. The mother is not free to enjoy and nurture her real child if her inner child is constantly interfering with the process. The father needs to strengthen his rational, adult state of mind so that it can stay in control and fend off intrusion by his envious inner child. Mother and father need to grow up. The psychological growth process is long and arduous, but it is necessary and its rewards are enormous.

Through the conflict with his wife, Johnny is again confronted with a choice: he can grow up and become a responsible adult capable of caring for another human being, or he can choose babydom and abandon his wife and young child. Many men leave.

DECEMBER 17

BLAME

BLAME is another hallmark of the narcissistic perspective. Consistent with the level of development of the young child is his inability to take responsibility for his behavior. Johnny blames his wife and accuses her of being dependent, needy, and demanding, instead of acknowledging his own self-absorption. If his wife is underdeveloped, she will accept his blame and consider the failed relationship her own fault; a child often blames herself for things that are not her fault.

The critical challenge for Johnny and his wife is to learn to stay in objective reality and behave in a manner that is appropriate to their chronological ages. The task is to reduce the margin between chronological age and psychological development.

If Johnny suffered an upbringing by abusive parents, his narcissism will be far more destructive than if he suffered the benign incompetence of well-meaning parents. Rather than choosing a submissive woman who will baby him, Johnny is more likely to choose a woman who will reenact the abusive patterns of his childhood with him. If he makes this choice, the abused Johnny has become the abusive Johnny, either by abusing someone else or himself. It is here that the connection between addictions and child abuse can be seen. If Johnny chooses to abuse himself, he will develop an addiction. He might become a substance abuser.

Drugs and alcohol simulate the infant's experience of fusion. The compulsion to get high is the regressive desire to return to a state of boundary-less merging with one's surroundings. It is the inner child's desire to return to a state of infantile bliss and wholeness—a time without pain, a time before the trauma of abuse. Regression is a flawed attempt to return to safety. No one can be an infant when he is not an infant. No attempt to return to a state of infancy can ever succeed because life's biological clock keeps ticking and nature forces chronological adulthood upon all of us. Any attempt at return is entirely futile, and the only possible result of trying is a chronological adult who behaves like an infant. Addictions are the inner child's maladaptive attempt to avoid the pain of his earlier trauma. Addictions are the silent movies that dramatize the situation of the child.

Abuse is a shattering experience for a child. It disrupts her entire growth process and destroys her natural inclination to trust. The infant is born physically and mentally whole. Abuse splinters the mind-body connection so that physical and emotional growth can no longer develop concurrently. The child's physical growth proceeds, but her emotional growth is interrupted. Abuse fragments the child twice. First it divides her body from her mind, and then it splits her developing personality into constructive and destructive components. Remember, children are not born destructive. They become destructive in response to destruction. Since new experiences create new passengers on the bus, the new passenger on the abused child's bus is the destructive child. Abuse has created the child's first injured inner child. This is the frightened inner child who longs to return to a time of safety before the abuse. The constructive child has a companion. The constructive child is hopeful, trusting, and happy, and like all living things, she seeks to survive. The destructive child is despairing, fearful, angry, and hurt. She is a victim who advocates regression. Her destructiveness and desire to regress are responses to her trauma. Her desire to regress differs from the natural resistance to psychological growth seen in the nurtured child. The difference is one of intensity. Some children grow up gracefully. Some children grow up kicking and screaming. Some children never grow up. The nurtured child responds to the demands for psychological growth with the least resistance. The nurtured child has the most freedom to develop the infrastructure necessary to become a rational adult. She is safe enough to learn. She can respond to the encouragement to grow because she trusts her caregivers. The child of incompetent parents resists psychological growth more strenuously because she is confused by mixed messages of the necessity to grow. Her parents unwittingly offer her the choice to stay a baby. The abused child is frozen in time. She is the child who refuses to grow up. Her world is too dangerous an environment for psychological growth. She is paralyzed with fear and stuck in the past at the time of her trauma. She is terrified of growth, and her only movement is backward. Her need for safety compels her to regress to a time when she was safe—a time before trauma, a time of wholeness. Wholeness is elemental to the human experience. The child is born whole. Trauma splits the child.

Addictions are ill-fated attempts to reunite with self. The biggest problem with addiction as a strategy for wholeness is that the fusion the addict longs for can never be accomplished from the outside with alcohol, drugs, food, or violence. The reunion must necessarily be from within. The next problem with addiction is that the "fix" it offers is entirely temporary. Healing is a permanent solution. Yet another problem with addiction is that it can provide only an illusion of safety for the addict. Any emotional regression to a time before trauma can deliver only an illusion of wholeness. It can never provide real wholeness. The objective reality of the physical world is not the same as the subjective reality of the emotional world. Addiction simply does not work. Only exposing and resolving the actual trauma that splintered the child will allow the reunion with self that is essential for healing and securing safety within.

If remembering the splintering trauma is necessary for healing, why is it so difficult to remember? Why is there so much resistance to a memory? The answer is twofold. First, the inner child confuses remembering with reexperiencing. The inner child lives in the subjective world of feelings, where thinking is the same as doing and remembering is the equivalent of reexperiencing. Adults enter this world regularly when they dream. In a dream state, the adult no longer distinguishes between reality and the dream. Second, the inner child needs to preserve the illusion that the caregiver he loves and trusts loves him back. This is a survival issue because the young child's life truly does depend on the caregiver. The young child cannot live without her. Denying the abuse is adaptive in early childhood but is extremely maladaptive in adulthood.

A rational adult understands that no one can turn a clock back. A rational adult understands that the past is the past. A child has no such developed concept of time. A child fears the past in the same way that an adult fears the events in his dreams. When a frightened inner child drives the bus, his decisions derive from fear. A frightened child will hide under a bed if the house is on fire, while a rational adult will try to escape. The frightened child perishes, and the rational adult survives. Addictions are the equivalent of hiding under a bed. They are the inner child's fearful solution to a problem that requires courageous adult action.

Addictions are the biggest obstacle constructed by the fearful inner child to avoid the pain of remembering his trauma and identifying his abuser. Addictions serve as immensely effective deflectors. As long as the individual is consumed by either satisfying his addiction or ridding himself of his addiction, he never looks at the purpose of his addiction. Addictions are thick screens that hide the trauma of abuse and the destructive intentions of the abuser. The intensity with which addictions persist is a reflection of the level of the fear of the inner child, who is terrified of reexperiencing his original trauma and identifying his abuser. For the inner child, exposing the abuser not only shatters his illusion of being loved, it also leaves the child vulnerable to retaliation. Remember, in the perceptual reality of the inner child, he is still at risk because time has stopped. The agenda of the frightened inner child is to block exposure of the original trauma and the identity of the perpetrator. His goal is to forget. The agenda of the constructive child is to remember because we learn from the past. When the needs of the constructive child clash with the needs of his destructive inner child, Civil War II rages internally. The abused child is at war with self. Who will prevail? Who will drive the bus?

Occasionally it is the constructive child who manages to find safety in her dangerous world. Against all odds, she drives the bus while her fearful, destructive inner child remains a passenger. In this unusual circumstance, the abused, frightened, angry inner child can remain silent for years until someone or something mobilizes her to seek control of the bus. She begins to remember, and memories start to surface. Unfortunately, it is usually the destructive inner child who then makes her way into the driver's seat, leaving the hopeful, constructive child sitting in the back of the bus fearful, alienated, and silent.

The destructiveness we witness in contemporary American society is rooted in childhood. It begins with trauma and the resulting internal struggle between constructive and destructive selves. It continues externally in clashes between parent and child, parent and adolescent, and then between adult and society. The struggle originates in childhood and advances into adulthood. Civil War II is a very real conflict with very real losses for the individual and for society.

LOSS AND ADDICTION

THE profound sense of loss experienced by abused children originates in the fragmenting of self that results from abuse. The child seeks to reunite with self. He seeks to become whole. He seeks to return to a time before abuse and pain. Addictions are ill-fated attempts to regain wholeness and avoid pain. Addictions cannot succeed because they are external; they require someone or something outside of self. Reunification with self is an entirely internal, intrapsychic process. The void the abused child feels can never be filled from outside with alcohol, drugs, food, or violence. It must be filled from inside by having self reunite with self to restore an integrated whole. The healing process is a reclamation project. Self-reunification begins with recognizing the trauma that caused the original split. The healing process provides a safe place for the inner child to tell his story instead of acting it out. It allows the splintered selves to understand their experience, feel their feelings, and reunite. Restoration of wholeness is the goal.

The disintegration of civilized life in America is

in direct proportion to the levels of child abuse in this country. The more abuse that occurs, the more destruction that is launched into society. The relationship is one of cause and effect. The destruction in our society cannot stop until its cause is acknowledged, understood, and healed. Safety begins at home. The American home must be safe for society to be safe.

The anger and despair characteristic of the destructive inner child translate into menacing behavior in society. The personal trauma of the abused child becomes society's trauma. Addiction is the legacy of child abuse, and the self-destruction that child abuse launches almost always includes destruction of others. The crime wave that accompanies substance abuse is a significant example. Whatever substance the abuser is addicted to costs money. When the angry, destructive inner child is driving the bus, he operates from the narcissistic principle of entitlement. "I want what I want when I want it." Since he has no boundaries, whatever the abuser wants he takes. Stealing is his way of life. His entitlement philosophy emboldens him to plunder.

What was annoying when Johnny was a child is dangerous now that Johnny is an adult. The snatcher is now a criminal. If he is armed with guns, knives, and other weapons of destruction, he is particularly menacing. Even though Johnny is a chronological adult, he remains a psychological child who has no remorse for his behavior. Johnny needs to be removed from society until he can develop a rational, responsible, adult state of mind that will control his urge to take what he wants when he wants it. Johnny needs to grow up. Since the effects of his underdevelopment are a danger to all around him, it is a survival decision to remove him from society. This action protects the responsible, law-abiding citizens at the expense of Johnny's freedom. Shall society empathize with Johnny for experiencing the trauma that caused his psychological growth to stop and his freedom to be restricted? Certainly. Shall society allow him to remain in society until such time as he can control himself? Certainly not. Johnny is a threat to civilized society and has a difficult challenge to meet. He must become self-aware. In order to heal, he must remember his trauma, identify the perpetrator, and understand his destructive response. He must train himself to think as a responsible adult. He must relinquish his inappropriate, regressive thinking patterns and grow up. This task will require Johnny to accept full responsibility for his behavior. He cannot blame anyone else for his choices but himself.

Blaming one's parents in this struggle is a common but useless strategy. It is each individual's responsibility to emerge from her own state of narcissism. If she did not accomplish this psychological growth concurrently with her physical growth, she can complete it out of sequence with a qualified therapist. Most people have less-than-ideal childhoods, so incompetent parents are not a valid defense for persistent narcissism. Blaming one's parents might feel good for the moment, but it accomplishes nothing and is a very convenient way to excuse oneself from doing the painful work of self-knowledge and psychological growth. Blame is an obstacle to growth. It keeps the blamer in a perpetual state of victimhood where she remains powerless. Powerlessness is useful to the blamer because it absolves her of any responsibility. Blamers enjoy the virtual reality of victimhood. In reality, the blamer's childhood is over and she is a chronological adult free to choose her path. But as long as she perceives herself as a victim, she can remain in a state of virtual powerlessness where she is not required to grow up. The social scientists and public officials who assign parental blame, genetic blame, or social blame for addictions and criminality sanction this state of virtual victimhood. They are unwittingly collaborating with the narcissist's quest to remain a victim. Responsible members of society must demand psychological adulthood from chronological adults. It is imperative that society expects and requires responsible, adult behavior from its citizens. If we abandon this standard, we are guilty of complicity in the establishment of a nation of frightened, angry children who refuse to become rational adults. We will have sanctioned a population that substitutes blame for responsibility, intentions for actions, and excuses for change.

Addiction is a response to trauma. Alcohol addictions, drug addictions, food addictions, and addictions to violence are maladaptations to the traumas of an abusive childhood. Addictive behavior is self-destructive on three levels. First, it can never succeed because unification of self is an entirely internal process. Second, it stalls the addicted individual in the past, in a perpetual state of regression where psychological growth is stopped. Third, it serves as a powerful deflector that shields the addict from facing his childhood trauma. Instead of expending energy to recognize his trauma, restart his emotional growth, and develop a rational, adult state of mind, the addict obsesses about his addiction. He focuses all his energy on either satisfying his addiction or defending it.

The most popular defense of addiction today is the hereditary defense. This is a particularly effective deflector used by both addict and apologists for the addict. The problem is that the heredity platform falsifies reality. It misrepresents trauma as genetics. It may be soothing to blame heredity for addictions in the short run, but it is completely subversive to the long-term healing process that requires self-knowledge. Blaming heredity, like blaming parents for behavior, keeps the addict in a perpetual state of powerless victimhood. Why would anyone prefer victimhood? What is the value of powerlessness? What is the purpose of addiction?

Addiction is an enormously powerful deflector used by the inner child to stay in control of the bus. This frightened inner child blurs time and space and holds the adult hostage. The inner child fears that the abuse will happen again. For him, remembering the trauma and experiencing the trauma are the same, and he will do anything to avoid the pain of reexperiencing the trauma. Addiction is the mask that disguises the trauma. As long as the terrified inner child can focus the attention on the mask, he will not have to feel the trauma of remembering. The struggle in addictions is between the chronological adult and his frightened inner child. Ironically, the adult has no idea who his adversary is. The adult believes that he is fighting a physical addiction. He does not realize that the addiction is a psychological war maneuver designed by his own terrified inner child. Addiction is a decoy whose purpose is to keep the adult too distracted to discover his childhood trauma. The addiction is a weapon of repression necessary to conceal his childhood trauma. Only when the mask is removed to expose the hidden trauma and the frightened inner child underneath, can the healing process succeed. In addictions, the frightened inner child is driving the bus.

What is the inner child so afraid of? The child has three basic fears. He fears being physically hurt, emotionally betrayed, and mentally out of touch with reality; that is, he fears pain, vulnerability, and insanity. These three fears continue to threaten his well-being throughout adulthood unless he remembers his trauma, identifies his abuser, and relinquishes his need to preserve his illusions. Abuse is always a threat to the child's physical safety that leaves him fearful. The more the child trusts the abuser, the more vulnerable he is and the more emotionally devastating and confusing the abuse. Abuse threatens the child's ability to test reality. The fear of insanity is both a fear of being out of control and of being out of touch with reality. The perpetrator threatens the child's perceptions of reality. Often the abuser tells the child that what happened did not happen. The abuser insists that the child is dreaming, imagining, or lying. Predictably, this is very confusing to a child and interferes with his developing sense of reality. Even when the abuser does not verbally threaten the child's perceptions of reality, the abuse itself is a threat to the child's reality, especially when the abuser is a trusted person. The child anticipates that the trusted person will help him, not hurt him. When the child gets hurt instead, he is bewildered.

Abuse is the most devastating when the abuser is the child's trusted caregiver, especially a parent. The young child's survival depends upon the caregiver. Somehow, the child must reconcile her simultaneous fear and need for the caregiver. The child has three options. First, she can deny the reality of the abuse to preserve her illusion that the caregiver loves her. In this instance, the child must deny her own perceptions of reality and accept unreality. This alternative endangers the child in the future when her survival depends upon herself and her accurate assessment of reality. Second, she can try to normalize the experience by converting her perception of pain to pleasure. That is, to preserve the illusion that her caregiver loves her, the child distorts her own reality and perceives her abuser as her advocate, not her enemy. This strategy leaves the child unable to accurately identify in the future who is her enemy and who is her advocate. In the third option, the child perceives the abuser as "not knowing" what he is doing. That is, the child cannot tolerate the reality that the trusted person is hurting her intentionally, so the child assumes that the perpetrator does not know. This option leaves the child open to fears that as an adult she too will be out of control and become abusive. After all, if the caregiver "didn't know," then the child is vulnerable to "not knowing" also.

Clearly, the illusion that the child is protecting is inevitably damaging to the child and to the adult he becomes. The fears and the distortions of reality that were necessary and adaptive for the abused child are hurtful to him in his adult life. They are the legacy of his abuse and interfere with his ability to make responsible choices for himself in adulthood. Only when the inner child of the adult he has become is physically safe and emotionally protected will he be able to speak about the abuse. Only then will he be able to relinquish the illusion that the caregiver "didn't know" and be free of his fears. The sooner the adult realizes that his abusers knew exactly what they were doing, the sooner the adult will be free of the need to distort reality and confuse advocate and enemy. He will be back in touch with objective reality where he is safe.

In all three strategies, the child's ability to test reality is compromised. The child learns to distrust her own perceptions. She develops fears of going crazy and not being able to distinguish real from unreal. Being in touch with objective reality, or knowing what is happening in the moment and being able to remember it, is an ongoing challenge for survivors of childhood sexual abuse, particularly when the abuser is trusted. Often in adulthood this translates into trusting other people's perceptions more than one's own. This chronological adult is particularly vulnerable to being manipulated by others. Giving away her trust in her own perceptions makes this individual easy prey for individuals or groups that will exploit her.

It may seem paradoxical that the inner child reenacts his trauma and at the same time attempts to repress his trauma through addictions. We can understand this apparent inconsistency by examining the state of mind of a frightened inner child. This child lives in the past where his trauma was real. Repressing the abuse makes sense for a frightened inner child who confuses the past with the present, who cannot distinguish between remembering and reexperiencing, and whose survival depends upon denying the abuse. The problem for the inner child is that the fear of remembering is in direct conflict with his constructive need to remember. The inner child wants to be safe and needs to be rescued. The silent inner child uses the encoded language of addiction to tell what happened to him. It is his cry for help. The inner child needs to come into the present where his adult self can understand his language and protect him. The adult must live in the present to rescue the inner child from the past.

The journey to free oneself from addiction is painful and long because it is a process of growing up that requires the adult state of mind to develop and take control. The individual embroiled in this battle fluctuates between self-loathing when her inner child prevails and self-pride when her adult triumphs. It is entirely predictable that this battle is erratic because growing up is never easy; it is always a struggle. The decision to recover is made by the adult state of mind. It is in direct conflict with the inner child who tries to subvert the recovery process because she needs to preserve the mask of addiction to disguise her trauma. Adults enter recovery programs with the same good intentions that motivate sincere individuals who enter psychotherapy programs. Each person attempts to recover and heal while under direct attack from her own inner child. The inner power struggle rages within, and the outcome of recovery and/or psychotherapy will be determined by the state of mind that prevails. The inner child wants to quit. The adult wants to persevere. In the most extreme cases of self-destruction, the inner child chooses death rather than the pain of remembering. She takes charge and commits suicide rather than face the painful knowledge of her childhood trauma. The profound sadness of suicide is that the inner child does not realize that her childhood is over. She functions on a very faulty premise. She would rather die than reexperience the abuse or confront her abuser. Sometimes she even feels that her suicide will finally punish her abuser. The child fantasizes that the abuser will be sorry. Her child's mind is not developed enough to know that the only escape from the abuser is reality.

Resistance to growth is a resistance to knowledge. The inner child confuses the knowledge of abuse with the abuse itself. The enduring tragedy of child abuse is that the trauma shuts the child down psychologically so that a rational adult does not develop. When the frightened inner child drives the bus, he continues to defend against reexperiencing abuse. Like the time-warping soldier, he believes that he is being threatened with abuse. If, for example, a child was abused in a basement, he may find himself fearful of basements as an adult. Every time he is required to descend into a basement he experiences anxiety and does not understand why. He might live his entire adult life simply avoiding basements, or he might experience enormous conflict because his life requires him to go into basements. If he is a detective or construction worker or simply lives in a house with a basement, he is repeatedly confronted with a perceptual threat to his safety. Only the adult state of mind is able to distinguish what is and what is not a real threat in reality, in the present.

The therapist must constantly mediate the individual's inner conflict and attempt to strengthen the adult state of mind to help the adult survive and stay in treatment. Only the adult state of mind can distinguish whether an inner child has usurped the steering wheel. The therapist helps the individual develop his rational, adult state of mind to a level that can stay in the present and provide safety for his inner child. The rational adult can reassure his inner child that the basement is safe and the abuser can no longer hurt the inner child. As long as the adult denies the abuse, the inner child is unheard and unsafe. As long as the inner child is afraid, the repression and addiction will continue. Addiction and repression are rooted in fears of the past intruding upon the present. To free oneself from addiction is to free oneself from the past. To choose growth is to choose life.

Both abusers and the abused resist the connection between childhood abuse and addiction. Why? The answer lies in the pain intrinsic to the growth process. Both abuser and abused are frozen in time by trauma. It is essential to understand that not all abused individuals become abusers, but it would be very difficult to find an abuser who was not at one time the abusee. Remember, children are not born violent; they become violent in response to the violence that is done to them. Regardless, it is the responsibility of the abuser to stop abusing. To accomplish this task requires the abuser to restart his psychological clock and grow up. He must leave the comfort of his excuses and do the painful work of developing a rational, adult state of mind. Similarly, it is the responsibility of the abused to stop tolerating the abuse. To accomplish this task requires the abused individual to restart her psychological clock and grow up. She must leave the familiarity of her powerless-victim position and develop a rational state of mind that will not tolerate being abused. The defense against abusing and being abused is the choice for psychological growth. It is the choice for self-knowledge. It is the choice for wholeness. It is the choice to survive.

The healing process for adult survivors of childhood sexual abuse is a reclamation project. The individual's fragmented selves are reintegrated, and reunion with self is accomplished. The traumatized, shut-down, frightened inner children are safe and secure. They are nurtured and protected by the adult the individual has become. Their experiences are accepted as part of the adult's history. Their fear and sadness is acknowledged as a reality of their trauma. Each inner child's existence is validated as a part of the adult's integrated, whole self. The adult listens to his inner children, but he remains in control of the bus. The ability to remain in objective reality is restored, and the needs for fear and distortion are eliminated. The individual is no longer tethered to the past. He is free and without addiction. His self-knowledge is complete.

Why do people resist the healing process? How can the freedom, independence, and autonomy of self-awareness be threatening? Self-awareness is only threatening to the vulnerable, frightened inner child who depends on her abuser for survival. She continues to live in the perceptual past where she cannot survive without her caretaker. As long as this inner child is driving the bus, she will sabotage the healing process because she needs her illusions. Therapy cannot dismantle her illusions until she has developed the adult infrastructure necessary to tolerate the information that her illusions are designed to hide. Therapy must proceed slowly and gently. If the frightened inner child refuses self-awareness, she will find herself with many options for expressing anger and re-creating the trauma of her childhood. Addictions to alcohol, drugs, food, or violence, are readily available vehicles designed to deflect attention away from her underlying trauma and keep it hidden.

SPOUSAL ABUSE

IF Johnny chooses to become an abuser, his wife is at risk. Spousal abuse is a complex interaction between husband and wife. Unlike the abused child, the wife is a chronological adult. She has choices. Spousal abuse presents the puzzling question of why the abused wife often chooses to stay in the relationship or chooses to return to the relationship after leaving. Her behavior is enigmatic. To explain the unexplainable, it is necessary to ask the question, "Who's driving the bus?" Like the stranded schoolboys in William Golding's *Lord of the Flies*, the wife's frightened inner child is driving her bus. When a frightened inner child is driving the bus of a chronological adult, that adult is vulnerable to the brutality of an aggressor in the same manner that a real child is vulnerable. If her fear paralyzes her, she will remain in an abusive relationship where she remains hopeful that her compliance will protect her. She is not psychologically developed enough to recognize the futility of her hopefulness. She functions psychologically as a powerless, frightened child despite her chronological age. What can free her?

The remedy for the disparity between chronological age and psychological functioning is the resumption of the learning process. The chronological adult must develop a rational, adult state of mind that is strong enough to overpower her own narcissistic inner child who still cowers in fear. The tragedy of the internal psychological battle between narcissism and adulthood is that when the inner child prevails, the chronological adult suffers. The irony for chronological adults in abusive relationships is that it is their own frightened inner children who imprison them. To be free, the abused wife must resume her psychological learning process. She must confront the reality of her childhood and grow up. It is her responsibility to herself and to her own survival. A qualified therapist can be of invaluable assistance in this process. The therapist acts as guide and advocate for the development of the wife's rational, adult state of mind. When the abused wife can identify where she is functioning on her time line, she has acquired the necessary skills to shift her state of mind from powerless inner child to powerful, rational adult. She is empowered by her knowledge of self. She has prevailed in her internal psychological battle between narcissism and responsible adulthood. The rational, adult state of mind does not tolerate abuse. She can leave. She is free, and it is her own psychological growth process that has freed her. Self-knowledge truly is power because it enables the individual to shift from the powerless position of the child to the powerful position of the rational adult. Although spousal abuse occurs more commonly from

husband to wife than from wife to husband, in either
situation it is the self-knowledge that empowers the
abused individual to move from the vulnerability of
childhood to the safety of adulthood.

The power of psychological adulthood is internal;
that is, the goal and achievement of psychological
adulthood is control of self. The psychological adult
seeks to control himself; the narcissist seeks to control
someone else. If Johnny chooses to become an abuser,
his children are at risk in his household. Johnny
may be reenacting the remembered brutality of his
own childhood, but his victims are his very real, very
innocent, very powerless children whom he is responsible for protecting. The fact that Johnny was abused
himself cannot excuse him from the reality that he
is now victimizing his own children. Johnny must be
stopped. If Johnny cannot stop himself, then it is society's responsibility to remove him. The alternative to
this course of action is in evidence today when abusive
parents are not held responsible for their behavior.
Social services are overwhelmed by families in crisis
that cannot escape the web of abuse. Abused children
are regularly returned to abusive homes where they
are beaten, raped, tortured, and even murdered.

Abused children need protection. The choices
available to a chronological adult are not available to
a child. The child is a prisoner of his environment
until he is old enough to leave. It is society's responsibility to protect its children and help them grow up.
Children must be removed from the grasp of abusive
parents. Emotional, physical, and sexual abuse are

human-rights violations. It is savage to return children to violent, abusive environments. Respect for human life demands that society not place parental rights above children's rights. The fundamental values that motivate social scientists and public officials to protect the rights of biological parents at the expense of the human rights of the child are so flawed, naive, and destructive that they must be redefined immediately. Retaining the nuclear family, regardless of the behavior of the nuclear family, is a flawed value implemented by well-intentioned social workers and the courts. An intact nuclear family is only an empty form; it is not a constructive goal in itself. An intact nuclear family that provides a safe, nurturing environment in which the children can grow is a constructive goal because it offers the content necessary for human growth. It is anathema to the growth process and to civilized life to force children to return to or remain in violent, abusive households. The human rights of children must prevail in the contest between the rights of the children and the biological rights of abusive parents.

Parents who abuse their children are reenacting their own abusive childhoods. Abusive parents are narcissists frozen in the past. Trauma has halted their psychological growth. Like a broken record, they keep repeating that trauma. Like any other criminal or addict, their recovery requires psychological growth and the movement from narcissism to rational adulthood. Recovery is the healing process that can reunite children with their families and citizens with society.

Only if the individual develops an adult, rational state of mind should she be permitted to reenter the community or should the children be allowed to go home. Committing oneself to recovery is the individual's responsibility.

HEREDITY DEFENSE

IT is fascinating that at this time in history a movement is gaining momentum that declares heredity to be responsible for destructive behavior, especially addictions. In this campaign, the individual is seen as the victim of his genetic destiny, one who cannot ethically be held responsible for something over which he has no control. The attraction of the heredity plea is that it absolves the addicted individual of any responsibility for his behavior. Genetic explanations for addictions are counterproductive because they misrepresent the root of addictions. Addictions are responses to trauma. They are the products of abuse, not genetics. Addictions serve the defensive purpose of deflecting attention away from the repressed trauma of child abuse, so that the trauma remains hidden. Addictions are the secret weapons of inner children. The inner child erects the barrier of addiction between herself and the chronological adult she has become. As long as the barrier remains intact, the chronological adult does not remember her childhood trauma. Even if she does remember the trauma, she will not make the connection between the childhood trauma and her adult behavior. If we acknowledge how powerful a force addiction is, we are beginning to grasp the nature of the intensity of the recovering addict's inner psychological battle. Her terrified inner child struggles to keep the abuse hidden, while her rational adult fights to end her addiction. Unconsciously, one part of her seeks to forget while the other part seeks to remember. The fearful inner child prevails when addictions continue.

The frightened inner child needs the addiction as a decoy to keep his rational adult occupied and away from the memories. The relapsing alcoholic's sorrow and remorse emanates from his adult state of mind that did not have the strength to withstand the incursion by his inner child. The food addict who cannot stop eating is similarly being overpowered by his inner child's demand to have what he wants when he wants it, regardless of the consequences. Against his better judgment, the rational adult surrenders to his inner child. It is sad that the rational adult does not understand the motive of the frightened inner child. Like the alcoholic, the food addict is engulfed by remorse and self-recrimination that serve to keep him occupied and away from the painful memories of his childhood trauma. It is very discouraging for these individuals when they lose their inner battles, but it is a complicated loss because the inner child welcomes it. A part of the individual feels victorious and a part of him feels defeated, depending upon who is driving the bus. The tragedy is that the chronological adult mistakenly believes that his war is against a substance or a behavior. He has no idea that he is warring against his own inner child, who is terrified of remembering his childhood trauma.

The individual who is addicted to violence is similarly mistaken. She cannot explain why she does what she does, only that she needs to do it. Her need to be violent emanates from the violence done to her. Her silenced inner child speaks when she reenacts the violence of her childhood and the rage and revenge she suppressed. The powerlessness she felt as the victim is transformed into the power she experiences while destroying someone or something else when she becomes the victimizer. Her angry inner child is driving the bus in this reenactment, and the boundaries of time and space have collapsed. The destructive inner child is not necessarily discriminating about what she destroys; she simply craves destruction. She must act out her story. She must express her rage. She is compelled to destroy. She is an addict.

Addiction is the Hallmark of Abuse

ADDICTION is the hallmark of abuse. It must be healed from the inside out with self-knowledge. Even if the individual can discipline himself to modify his behavior, his addiction will resurface in another form until he recognizes and resolves the underlying trauma. "Addictive" personalities are not born; they are made. Destruction is a learned behavior. Clarifying that this battle is internal is extremely useful because it is so much easier to fight a known enemy. Addiction counselors who can help a client recognize his internal saboteur have helped that client defend against internal attack. If the individual accepts self-knowledge as his goal and recognizes that a part of himself seeks to sabotage that goal, that individual is far better equipped to manage his inner conflict than the person who does not know that the saboteur exists within. If society sanctions the demands of the inner child to forget, then the saboteur has an external partner. The individual feels internal pressure from his inner child and external permission from society to remain unconscious of childhood trauma. It is critical for the individual's growth process that society recognizes this dynamic and refuses to become an unwitting accomplice of the self-sabotaging inner child. It is also crucial for the safety of society because the individual's internal battle will eventually become society's nightmare. Crime is the external manifestation of the addict's internal battle.

It is convenient but extremely counterproductive for society to accept addictions as an issue of heredity. Responsible society needs to expose the secret weapons of the relentless inner child and refuse to become her accomplice. Addictions are first a barricade to self-knowledge and second an attempt to recapture the reverie of fusion that characterizes the state of infantile narcissism—a time before trauma. In contrast to the separateness and personal empowerment that accompanies growth and development, addictions are regressive attempts to return to boundary-less infancy, attempts to recapture a time of rapture. Addictions are dependent behaviors that recall a time of life when the baby felt safe and could not distinguish between self and other. Whether the individual chooses to blur her boundaries through the high of drugs and alcohol, the comforts of food, or the drama of violence, when the behavior is an addiction it is maladaptive. In the inner child's arsenal, addictions are the most powerful weapons for forgetting. An individual who chooses rational adulthood does not become addicted. Addictions are the pathetic spoils of the victory of the frightened inner child. The adult remembers; the child forgets.

UNCONDITIONAL LOVE

WHAT is appropriate dependency in infancy and early childhood is entirely maladaptive in later life. Addictive behaviors that seek to annihilate the boundaries between self and other, or self and the outside world, are self-destructive, regressive behaviors. When the boundaries between self and other, and self and the world, are obliterated, the individual ceases to function or live in the real world. The state of being boundary-less that is natural to the infant pronounces the chronological adult functionally dead. The unconditional love and acceptance of the infant that is appropriate to infancy is also maladaptive in later life. The unconditional acceptance and love that is demanded by the narcissist is the hallmark of his addiction. "Love me, love all of me." "Accept me, accept all of me." Why? Why should any rational adult accept this narcissistic ultimatum from anyone but an infant? He should not. Why should any society accept this narcissistic ultimatum from its citizens? It should not.

The unconditional-love enthusiasts invoke the

heredity plea in their defense. They argue that since they are the products of their genes, society should accept their behavior as a natural yield of the gene pool. The I-was-born-that-way platform argues that an individual's behavior is her inheritance, not her choice. The individual is the victim of her genetic destiny and cannot ethically be held responsible for something she has no control over. The narcissistic attitude is especially creative in this arena because it seeks to engage the sympathy of the parent portion of the rational adult. The parent portion of the rational adult has two dimensions: one internal and one external. Both are passengers on the bus. The external parent is the mother or father who is visible, the one Johnny introduces as Mom or Dad. The internal parent is the inner unseen, emotional counterpart of the external parent. The inner parent is vulnerable to Johnny's charms. The external parent is motivated by reason and remains impervious to Johnny's manipulations. It is the inner parent who must be developed enough to help Johnny emerge from his state of narcissism. The narcissist's position of strength in this debate is to target the sympathetic inner parent, rather than the objective, rational, external parent who remains in an adult state of mind. If Johnny can engage and convince the inner parent that he should not be held responsible for his behavior, the inner parent becomes Johnny's accomplice and advocates his irresponsibility. The inner parent may even go to the extent of feeling responsible for Johnny's behavior because, after all, the child is the parent's offspring. The power of Johnny's argument is directly proportional to the guilt he can induce in the inner parent. If the inner parent remains unmoved and stays in a rational, adult state of mind, he will hear the glaring flaw in Johnny's argument. The error is Johnny's assumption that behavior is a fixed characteristic like eye color or skin color. The narcissist claims, "I was born that way!" So what? What is the connection between present behavior and past behavior? All human life begins in a state of narcissism, yet not all human beings end as addicted narcissists. What happens in between is a matter of choice. If the rational adults in society can be persuaded to view behavior as a fixed entity, then they have accepted the narcissists' contention that heredity, not choice, determines behavior.

RESPONSIBLE LEADERSHIP

THE war between the inner child's narcissistic state of mind and the rational adult's state of mind continues in America. When government sanctions regression, the inner child has a potent, external ally in his internal campaign to deny and forget the abuse. Without the encouragement of a rational adult, why would any child grow up and become self-aware? It is the rational adult who presents responsible adulthood as the goal of childhood. When parents abdicate this responsibility in their families and governments abdicate this responsibility in society, the goal of self-sufficiency is lost and we are left with a community of narcissistic adults commanded by their frightened, needy inner children. Children need responsible parents, and society needs responsible governments. Responsible leadership in both the private and public sectors is achieved through the individual psychological growth process of the parent and public official, respectively. In each case, civilized life requires its leaders to emerge from narcissism into responsible adulthood. Society needs chronological adults who are self-aware, psychological adults. With comprehensive adulthood as the goal of childhood, the standard for evaluating behavior becomes a simple dichotomy. That which promotes psychological growth is positive; that which promotes regression is negative. Any decision that promotes psychological growth promotes life and is constructive. Any decision that promotes regression promotes death and is destructive. In the narcissistic world of chaos and infantile adults, productive life ceases to exist. A society dominated by out-of-control inner children cannot survive.

NARCISSISM IS UNIVERSAL

THE narcissistic attitude is universal. Since all human beings are born into a state of total narcissism, and all are presented with the same developmental task of emerging from this state of narcissism into rational adulthood, we universally share the challenge of growing up. The narcissistic attitude is a pervasive state of mind that defies any classification. It is the comprehensive nature of narcissism that makes it so threatening and hard to see. Narcissism is a natural human trait appropriate to infancy and early childhood. Overcoming one's primitive state of narcissism is the requirement for civilized life in any society.

The struggle begins within self when the first limits are placed upon Johnny's behavior. When Johnny is admonished for snatching his playmate's toy, the responsible adult is placing limits upon Johnny. If Johnny succeeds in developing a healthy respect for his own boundaries, he can then respect his playmate's boundaries and give back the toy. He has a choice. If he internalizes this lesson, he is on his way to becoming a responsible adult. As Johnny grows up physically, he will continually be presented with the psychological choice of narcissism or adulthood, regression or growth, past or present. The more he chooses adulthood, the stronger the development of his rational, adult state of mind. The more he chooses narcissism, the weaker his adult state of mind. Which attitude prevails in this struggle is determined by Johnny's choices. Who will be driving Johnny's bus is ultimately up to Johnny.

Taking responsibility for his own choices is Johnny's position of power. Blame is the position of powerlessness. When adult Johnny blames his behavior on his parents, his friends, his genetics, his god, or his government, he identifies himself as the powerless child of his childhood. If public institutions sanction Johnny's blaming, they have helped sabotage Johnny's growth process and encouraged his narcissism. Sociologists, psychologists, politicians, scientists, and theologians who blame the family, the system, genetics, and a lack of prayer all overlook Johnny's contribution to his own outcome. Personal responsibility is the attitude of the responsible adult; blame is the attitude of the narcissist.

Strengthening the family and improving the system are essential social and political goals. Adult Johnny must not, however, be permitted to excuse his current behavior because of inadequacies in his family or the system. Johnny's religious life is not liable for his behavior either. Strengthening Johnny's religious commitment is helpful only if Johnny is going to pray for the strength he needs to undertake the difficult internal work of growing up and becoming self-aware. If prayer fortifies his commitment to his own growth process, then it is useful. If prayer is used to absolve Johnny of his personal responsibility to grow and his god becomes the responsible party, then prayer is being used to blame his god for Johnny's behavior; that is, he will claim that his god did not answer his prayers. Psychological growth crosses all religious, cultural, sexual, age, and economic boundaries. Psychological growth is the universal challenge of human life.

If Johnny's psychological growth is frozen by trauma, he can easily become a career narcissist—an addict paralyzed by fear, driven by his terrified inner child, completely unaware of his need to repress his trauma. When abuse shatters a child, the natural narcissism of early childhood is transformed into the rigid, unremitting need to repress the trauma and avoid pain. Yet the silenced inner child continues to speak in the encoded language of his reenactments. It is in this way that addictions are created. Even when psychological growth stops, biological growth continues and we are left with chronological adults who behave like out-of-control children. When the inner children are driving the buses, society is out of control. Neither prayer, jails, nor blame can help us. Only we can help ourselves. We need to demand self-awareness and responsible adult behavior. We need to develop our rational, adult states of mind. We need to grow up.

REGAINING CONTROL OF THE BUS

EMOTIONALLY, the narcissistic adult is an underdeveloped child. The inner battle for control of the narcissist's mind is waged between his powerful inner child and his tentative, developing adult. The hallmark of the narcissist is that his inner child has prevailed. In contrast, the responsible adult wins the inner battle for control of the mind. Restraint and the ability to delay gratification are the hallmarks of rational adulthood. Evidence of this inner battle and its consequences is in every decision that is made by any individual at any given time in his life. "Who's driving the bus?" is a pervasive question. It is a comprehensive worldview involving every relationship and interaction in the individual's life. It is because of its pervasiveness that this battle is so crucial. All behavior derives from it. Thought precedes behavior, even if the thought is not rational. So, to answer the puzzling question of why society is so out of control, one must first answer the question "Who's driving the bus?" If it is one of the inner children, the task to regain control begins with removing the individual's inner child from the driver's seat and having his rational adult take over. If the individual is unwilling to change seats, or unable to because he has no rational adult developed enough to take over, he will remain in a perpetual state of narcissism and his battle between self and other will begin. The narcissistic adult abandons his inner struggle and goes out into society to wage an external war against responsible adults over control of society's bus. Rather than do the work of internal growth, the narcissist demands that society change. Instead of personal change he demands social change.

Merit-based performance is not relevant to the narcissist. She demands accolades without doing the work. Any time society collaborates by awarding advancement without performance, society has undermined its own survival. If schools award diplomas to unqualified students, they have entered the world of feelings and fantasy and have abandoned the world of facts, performance, rational thought, and the meritocracy. If a diploma is awarded to a student who has not earned it to prevent that student from feeling bad, the school has discredited itself and participated in its own destruction. Diplomas from schools that graduate unqualified students punish the hard-working students who have done their work because the diplomas no longer represent competence. Worthless diplomas do not change reality. Untrained graduates are unemployable no matter what their diplomas say.

Only in the narcissistic world of fantasy do feelings and intentions have the same value as actual performance. Children confuse thinking and doing; rational adults do not.

When the narcissistic attitude invades the educational system, standards for achievement are lowered to artificially bolster the student's self esteem. This is extremely damaging to the perception of objective reality and is subversive to the learning process. When performance standards are lowered and requirements are reduced, students feel great about themselves only as long as they remain inside the virtual reality of their artificially controlled environment. When they leave and are confronted with the real, competitive world, their self-esteems plummet because they are not as qualified as they perceived themselves to be. They are confused and angry. In this situation, they have two choices. They can pursue internal change by disciplining themselves to study and acquire the skills they need to be competitive in the real world, or they can demand external, social change. That is, they demand an extension of their virtual reality to the workplace where employees are hired on the basis of need, not skill. The choice for internal change involves growth and is the appropriate adaptation to the demands of objective reality. The external change demanded by the narcissist to dismantle the meritocracy is regressive. It seeks to change the adult reality of the necessity for performance and replace it with the child's need to feel good. Incompetent students and workers are as ineffective as incompetent parents.

Competence is the source of self-esteem. In objective reality, performance is not confused with intentions and thinking is not confused with doing. Worthless diplomas and undeserved hiring do not enhance self-esteem; they impede the individual's growth process and retard the productivity of society.

In every sphere of American life, the narcissistic individual, driven by his narcissistic inner child, seeks to dominate responsible citizens. The narcissist's agenda is to promote his need-based standard of behavior, which is diametrically opposed to the merit-based standard of the rational adult. The narcissist is entirely committed to his need-based philosophy. He defends it passionately and eloquently because it flows naturally from his infantile belief system: "because I need it, I am necessarily entitled to it." His attitude is appropriate in infancy and childhood. The infant needs food, so he is entitled to be fed. The infant needs shelter, so he is entitled to be clothed and housed. The failing of this belief system is when it is inappropriately applied to chronological adults. Narcissism is the natural state of infancy because the baby is totally dependent and without boundaries. Children are born narcissistic. They are not born "bad." It is when narcissism advances into adolescence and adulthood that it becomes negative. Unrestrained narcissism is an insidious threat to civilized life because its power base is hidden within. It is an ongoing battle within each individual that must be fought with vigilance and knowledge.

If the regressive, narcissistic state of mind remains

unchallenged and is allowed to overpower the rational, adult state of mind, narcissistic individuals will eventually increase and outnumber the rational adults in society. If this happens, we will witness the total collapse of American society because a majority of narcissists will overpower a minority of rational adults externally in the real world. The internal battle will be lost to the inner child and will be translated into the lost external battle in society. What steps can we take in the external world to strengthen our infrastructure against incursion by advancing narcissistic adults?

RECOGNIZING THE NARCISSIST

FIRST we must identify the narcissist. One obstacle to recognizing the narcissist is that she is often very highly developed in many areas of her life. She is disguised as a responsible adult. Individuals who have attained extremely high positions in the workplace, politics, or academics can at the same time be extremely underdeveloped psychologically. Parents who abuse the children in their care are often well-educated, well-dressed narcissists in disguise. The child abuser is usually not the stereotypical stranger in a raincoat whom we teach our children to fear. More often the child abuser is a person the child knows and trusts: his parent, stepparent, grandparent, babysitter, doctor, teacher, coach, clergy member. "Who can you trust?" is not an easily answered question. Narcissism is extraordinarily varied in its self-expression and intensity. The rational adult does not always recognize the disguised narcissist. The narcissist is a chameleon. She disguises herself in various roles of respectability. The rational adult remembers that the person, not her facade, must be evaluated.

If a politician is a disguised narcissist, his leadership will reflect the narcissistic perspective of self-absorption. His inability to value other opinions will render him unable to compromise effectively. If his self-absorption corrupts his integrity, he might abuse his power by accepting bribes. The narcissist does not honor commitments. He places his personal agenda above the public promises he makes to his constituency. He "forgets" his promises. This is not a conflict of interest for the narcissist. There is no conflict; he comes first. If voters do not want to be victimized by the narcissistic politician, they must grow up themselves and vote responsibly. They must assess the candidate on his record, not his promises. The rational adult remembers to evaluate the person, not the facade.

Narcissism is the enemy of growth, but the narcissist is not always seen as the enemy. Sometimes he is charming and lovable and only expresses his narcissism in extremely isolated circumstances. The kind, gentle, hard-working husband who flies into rages is a disguised narcissist. His behavior confuses his wife because he is so good to her in many respects. Because she loves the kind, gentle side of him, she may tolerate the rages even if he is physically abusive. The wife denies or ignores his abusive side in the childish hope that he will change. She tries not to provoke his anger but is unsuccessful. When the wife accepts his abuse, she conspires with the husband's inner child because children are not held responsible for their behavior. Why should the husband change? Why should he control his angry inner child if his wife accepts being abused? The issue in spousal abuse is that the husband's inner child is out of control, and the wife's inner child is powerless to stop the assault. Both have their inner children driving the buses, and each needs a rational, adult state of mind to take control of the wheel. The wife who does not want to be victimized by a narcissistic husband must grow up and leave.

Often narcissism is unrecognized for what it is. If a judge is a disguised narcissist, his decisions will be sympathetic to the narcissistic perspective of blame. In his courtroom, abusive behavior will be blamed on society or the family and an impoverished childhood. The victimizer will be seen as the victim and will not be held personally responsible for his behavior. He will be released back into the community and continue his narcissistic, antisocial behavior patterns. It is difficult to acknowledge the destruction that accompanies the narcissistic individual. His negative behavior is given a myriad of explanations and excuses, none of which correctly identifies a lack of psychological development. The narcissist needs intervention whether he is the criminal or the judge; in either case, his behavior has negative consequences.

If a psychologist or social worker is a disguised narcissist, her interpretations will reflect the narcissistic perspective of helplessness. She becomes the unwitting accomplice of the client's regressive inner child. Her professional advice validates the continuing sense of victimization experienced by the client. The "poor Johnny" approach to psychotherapy sabotages the growth process. Johnny's developing adult state of mind needs an advocate for growth. His regressive inner child needs to be restrained. In each case the abuses of power by the disguised narcissist—whether psychologist, husband, wife, judge, social worker, politician, parent, or caretaker—are driven by the regressive force of his own inner child, which also needs to be restrained.

APPROPRIATE TIMES FOR REGRESSION

A state of mind is fluid, so even a well-developed, rational adult can behave narcissistically in a time of crisis. Following death, divorce, job loss, illness, or any of life's crises, the individual may experience a time of regressive functioning. A time of adjustment to a new reality is predictable and not problematic. Another circumstance in which regression is appropriate is when the rational adult wants to play. It is important to understand that the playful inner child is also a passenger on the bus. When the playful child is out, the rational adult has fun. He can relax, enjoy sports, make jokes, play games, and have sex. The playful child, the inquisitive child, the affectionate child, and the happy child are all passengers on the bus. They enrich our lives with their sense of wonderment and hope. The problem in our society is not the rational individual in crisis or the rational adult at play. The problem in our society is the career narcissist who consistently has his angry, frightened inner child driving his bus. This entity is extremely dangerous to others. Child abusers, rapists, murderers, and torturers are all career narcissists who ravage those around them. It is very confusing to society that any human being can be so vicious and destructive to another, especially when the victim is a child.

If we examine the mind of the career narcissist, we can understand that he time-warps between past and present. At the time when he is the most destructive, his most angry inner child is in command. The damage a child can do in his imagination is equivalent to what an armed, chronological adult can do in reality. The consequences of this combination are devastating. The career narcissist must first be identified and then removed from society until he can develop and strengthen his rational, adult state of mind to a level where it can stay in control of his angry inner children. If he remains a career narcissist permanently, he must be removed from society permanently. An angry inner child unleashed into society as a chronological adult is the unacceptable alternative. It is imperative for the safety of our society that social scientists and civil libertarians understand that this is not a civil rights issue; it is a safety issue for society in general. Law-abiding citizens are entitled to a life free of the ravages of out-of-control, time-warping individuals whose frightened, angry inner children are driving their buses.

Recognizing that this dynamic exists within the mind is the first step toward remedying the problem. Understanding that career narcissists may look like responsible citizens but do not behave like responsible adults is the next task. It is very threatening to the rational adults in society when they realize that the enemy is not easily identified. Doctors, lawyers, psychologists, social workers, judges, teachers, coaches, parents, grandparents, aunts, uncles, sisters, brothers, baby-sitters, day-care workers, friends, neighbors—all are possible career narcissists capable of shattering those around themselves. They lie, deny, blame, forget, and distort reality. Career narcissists are revisionists who victimize others and then seek to avoid the consequences. When cornered, they often plead ignorance or insanity. Civilized America must disarm them. We must refuse to unwittingly become their accomplices by denying that they exist or by making excuses for their behavior. We must expose the disguised narcissists by recognizing their disguises. We must acknowledge Civil War II and remember that it is a war between states of mind. First internally and then externally, we must remember that narcissism is the enemy of rational adulthood. We must never forget that remaining in adult, rational states of mind is an ongoing challenge for all of us as long as we live. We must demand rational adulthood from ourselves. Only then will we be strong enough to demand rational adulthood from the career narcissist and remove him from society until he attains it. The capacity for personal, individual growth exists within each of us. We simply must do the internal work and grow up psychologically.

STEPS FOR INDIVIDUAL GROWTH

THE steps for individual growth begin with a commitment to psychological growth and development. They include recognition of the multiple states of our minds and a commitment to a program of self-monitoring that identifies who is driving the bus at all times. Individual growth demands that we each take personal responsibility for all of our behaviors and for every passenger on our bus. The steps for individual, internal growth must be extended to society so that we treat others with the same respect with which rational adults treat themselves.

In adulthood, it is the merit system that must prevail for society to flourish. The most qualified student, the most qualified job candidate, the most qualified politician, the most qualified anyone must be the individual who is rewarded with advancement. If the merit system is replaced by the need-based system, the neediest student, the neediest job candidate, the neediest politician, the neediest anyone is rewarded with advancement. In this system, the most unproductive are rewarded at the expense of the most accomplished. It is not difficult to imagine the eventualities of such a system. If merit is replaced with need as an incentive, then being the neediest becomes the goal for advancement. All progress halts as society adjusts to being upside down. What was valued becomes disvalued. What was unacceptable becomes acceptable. In this upside-down, need-based society, the inner children are in control. They have wrested the power from the well-meaning adults who were unable to recognize the narcissist's agenda for what it was: a power struggle for control. This conflict will escalate when well-intentioned adults realize that their own complicity in the war against themselves has emboldened the narcissistic enemy who seeks to destroy all semblance of rational, orderly life. The narcissist seeks to destroy civilized society as we know it in his consuming need to be loved unconditionally, accepted unconditionally, and employed unconditionally.

Rational adults must recognize their complicity in the assault against themselves and their standards of behavior. When an adult makes excuses for the unacceptable behavior of his spouse, his child, his coworker, or himself, he has conspired to dismantle the meritocracy. Excuses prolong and protect the narcissistic attitude of the emotionally underdeveloped. When parents swoop down to catch a child before he falls, they are unwittingly interrupting the growth cycle of that child. The child needs to learn causality, a basic premise for rational thought and decision-making. He needs to experience the natural consequences of his choices. He must learn the cause and effect of life: if he studies he will learn, if he practices he will improve, if he chooses not to study he will fail. When parents make excuses for Johnny's behavior and blame the teacher for his failure, the parents have subverted the learning process by not allowing Johnny to feel the natural and logical consequences of his choices. The parents artificially try to alter the child's environment rather than allowing the child to learn to adapt to the demands of reality. Rather than promote responsibility, they unintentionally sanction his narcissism.

Similarly, our well-intentioned government is interfering with society's growth process by federally dismantling the meritocracy and substituting national need-based systems. The welfare system in this country must be restructured so that the goals of self-sufficiency and adulthood are encouraged rather than subverted. In today's system, the incentive for reward is often to be unproductive. Second and third-generation welfare is an atrocity. It completely subverts its stated purpose. Welfare was designed and originally implemented as crisis intervention, but it has become a way of life for many. Why should anyone work and pay taxes when the government will support her for not working? Why should anyone marry when the government will give aid to dependent children only when one is not married? Why should anyone grow up if growth is not demanded of her? The government's culpability in the collapse of society's meritocracy is obscured by good intentions. The government's social programs are unwittingly designed to undermine the family—the single most important structure in civilized society. In the same way that the well-meaning parent swoops down to rescue the child, the well-meaning government swoops down to rescue citizens who need to become self-sufficient, not more dependent. Even the language used in these programs is offensive to the rational adult. *Entitlements.* What does that word mean? Is the government suggesting that adults are entitled to the same level of support to which infants are entitled? Why is that? Why is any adult entitled to any support from the government at all? Clearly, in order for society to flourish and grow, we need independent, autonomous adults who work and produce. Encouraging unproductiveness is so foolhardy it is hard to understand on what basis the idea was conceived. The narcissistic, need-based world of infancy and childhood must never be permitted to become the standard of behavior for adults.

HALTING CURRENT TRENDS

TO halt the current trends that are dismantling the merit system and threatening our way of life, responsible citizens will have to recognize these trends as serious threats. When the silent majority is mobilized, it has the power to demand that government programs be redesigned and restructured with productivity as the stated goal. Any program that encourages unproductiveness must be abandoned. Individuals within themselves, parents with their children, and governments with their citizens must necessarily have rational adulthood as the goal. Programs and decisions, strategies, and disbursements must have the emergence from narcissism and the entry into responsible adulthood as the stated purpose. Individuals, parents, and governments need not be apologetic or timid in this call for action. Narcissism is the absolute enemy of responsible adulthood and civilized society. It needs to be identified and eliminated—gently in the teachings of childhood, but rigorously in terms of adults fighting their inner battles and governments trying to solve domestic problems at the federal, state, and local levels. Personal responsibility must become the standard of behavior. No excuses.

Only in infancy and early childhood can we afford to accept the unacceptable. It is imperative that as soon as a child is able to distinguish between fantasy and reality, efforts are made to keep him in objective reality. This reality-based training will serve him and society very well. Objective reality teaches us that behavior is more valuable than motives. If a mother says that she loves her child but neglects him, which shall we believe? What she says or what she does? Does it matter why she does not feed him if he is starving? Should we excuse the inexcusable because the mother was reenacting the suffering of her own deprived childhood? In a reality-based society, motives are not confused with behavior, intentions do not substitute for actions, and explanations are not accepted as excuses. Motives are important only insofar as they are instructive in changing behavior. If the mother can understand why she deprived her child, then she is in a better position to change her behavior. If she is too underdeveloped psychologically to care for a child, then someone else must take care of the child. The biological rights of the mother are not primary; the human rights of the child must prevail.

No Excuses

THE social service system in this country needs to be restructured to help provide for the growth and development of its citizens, while at the same time recognizing that an emotional baby cannot adequately care for a real baby. Children are dying in America because social services have not asked themselves the question, "Who's driving the bus?" If an addicted mother is abusing her child, she needs help developing the inner, psychologically responsible adult necessary to adequately care for her own child. And in the meantime, while her deprived inner child is driving her bus, her real child must be removed from her care. Every individual must be held responsible for the consequences of her choices, period. No excuses.

The insanity defense, frequently used to excuse the inexcusable, is seriously flawed because it does not constructively acknowledge and address the fluid nature of an individual's state of mind. The insanity defense needs to be abandoned. If an individual brutalizes another, whether it be a spouse, a child, or a stranger, that individual must bear the consequences.

There can be no insanity plea that argues the individual did not know what he was doing at the moment. No excuses. If an angry inner child was driving the bus at that moment, it is still the individual's responsibility to bear the consequences for the actions of every passenger on his bus, including that angry inner child. No excuses. America must necessarily be a society of personal responsibility, or the unacceptable will become acceptable. Self-awareness is the work that introduces our most developed self to our inner children. We must meet them and acknowledge their existence within us.

If the most developed adult part of our personality is not held personally accountable for all of our actions, the ramifications are enormous. Any individual can present himself as fragmented and then never be held accountable for the actions of any unruly part of his own personality. In this chaotic scenario, the regressive inner child of the narcissist has prevailed; his demand for unconditional acceptance has been honored. "Love me, love all of me" is his anthem. Feelings become more important than behavior. "My angry inner child was driving the bus." "I was upset." "I was jealous." "I was tired." "I was overwhelmed." "I could not help it." The angry inner child has a thousand excuses for his inexcusable behavior. The battering husband, the abusive parent, the cruel teacher—they can all hide behind the narcissistic demand for total acceptance when society accepts the behavior of their angry inner children and the havoc that they wreak.

JUST SAY NO

DEAR America, it is time for the responsible adults among us to say *no*. No, I will not accept the unacceptable. No, I will not accept the demand for unconditional acceptance and love from anyone except an infant. No, I will not hand over the bus keys to a child. No, I will not surrender my power to the demands of a narcissist. I can see that a narcissist is a frightened, angry inner child, disguised as an adult. I will not relinquish my power to my own inner children or to anyone else's. Enough. I will not participate in the dismantling of civilized society.

Personal responsibility rests on the foundation of objective reality and rational thought. In objective reality, we are who we are at the present moment. If an inner child is driving the bus we must still be held accountable for that child's actions—period. No excuses. How can we implement a reality-based system of rational thought where rational adults are in charge?

First, we must be a society committed to a standard of behavior to which all citizens adhere. We must demand from every member of society that he be responsible for any and all of his actions regardless of who is driving his bus at the moment. No exceptions. No excuses. Second, we must commit ourselves to a system of self-examination that begins by asking the question, "Who's driving the bus?" In this way, we will be able to monitor our states of mind and help ourselves stay in rational, adult states of mind. If the adult is not strong enough or developed enough to take command of the bus, we must commit ourselves to a program of personal growth and development through education and/or psychotherapy. We must grow up psychologically. If we have not grown up in the ideal, natural, chronological sequence of life, we can grow up with a qualified therapist. To emerge from our narcissism into states of rational adulthood, we must learn to identify and become familiar with all the passengers on the bus. Self-knowledge is essential. We must become familiar with our own inner children. This is an enormous challenge but an absolute necessity. It is in pursuit of this goal that society should spend its resources. It is only through self-knowledge that lasting change can take place. It is only through the process of growth and development that we can eventually realize the dream of a civilized society of peace and harmony. Peace is possible only in a place where responsible adults have the power. Children can never be allowed to rule; their narcissistic agendas are simply not conducive to harmonious living. It is a certainty that a person without boundaries cannot live in peace with a person with boundaries. The nature of the one without boundaries is that she will try to intrude upon the one with boundaries. This is the principle that underlies the power struggle of an individual's inner child with her rational adult, of parents with their children, and the ongoing conflict in society between the narcissists and the responsible adults.

Narcissism must never be confused with rational self-interest. The goal of the narcissist is unconditional acceptance and a return to the entitlements of infancy. The narcissist perceives all demands and restrictions on him as excessive and punitive. Rational self-interest is a very different matter. Rational self-interest is rooted in the philosophy that "I am an important and valuable human being. I am as important to myself as my neighbor is to himself." What distinguishes rational self-interest from narcissism is the ability to differentiate self from other. Central to this is the acknowledgment that "my neighbor is as important to himself as I am to myself." This acknowledgment is entirely lacking in the narcissist. It is what puts the narcissist in direct opposition to the responsible adult in society. It is the basis for Civil War II. What can we do to resolve the conflict?

It is impossible to change what is not known, so the first step in change is defining the problem. We must identify the players. Self-monitoring and knowing the passengers on the bus are essential elements of self-definition. If we can ask ourselves or allow someone else to ask, "Who's driving the bus?" we have a tool to help us understand our behavior. Asking the question focuses the questioner's attention on the driver's identity. We can verify whether one of our inner children is in control. When one of our inner children is driving, we are in a state of regression. This is the first thing that must be remedied. Whether it is a playful inner child and it is not time to play or an angry inner child and it is inappropriate to express anger, it is time for the most developed adult to explain gently to that child that the adult is going to drive. The child is gently moved to a passenger seat, and the adult takes the wheel. This internal interaction may appear contrived and awkward at first, but it is an excellent exercise for identifying which state of mind is in control. Since we know that behavior proceeds from thought, once the adult is seated at the wheel we can be confident that decisions regarding behavior will flow from the most adult part of us rather than from the most childish part. This is a good beginning. Self-monitoring is a necessary skill that must be used in the internal and external war against narcissism. Since behavior derives from thought and thought is determined by who is driving the bus, it is critical to know who is driving at all times.

Once the rational adult driver has replaced the inner child, clear thinking is restored and the individual has left the world of feelings and returned to the world of thought. It is important to remember that all the passengers on the bus are entitled to influence the adult driver; they just cannot be allowed to drive. Inner children are like lobbyists. They urge legislation that will advance their particular agendas, but it is necessary for the decision maker to remember the broad interests of growth so that he will not be seduced by the special interests of one group. Self-knowledge derives from education. As long as a person acquires the tools, it is not critical whether he learns these lessons from a loving, responsible parent; qualified therapist; teacher; or mentor committed to the ideals of growth. Whether a baby is nourished at the breast or bottle is not critical as long as he gets the food he needs to survive. Without the food he will die. Without the tools of survival, society will die. The civil war between the states of mind is a war of survival.

Choosing Life

THINGS never stay the same in life; they either get better or worse. At this moment in history the quality of life in our nation is disintegrating because our society is being overrun with narcissistic adults who are trying to seize power from responsible adults. To reverse this trend and rechart the course toward growth and self-sufficiency, the responsible adults in our society need to confront the narcissism that is threatening to overwhelm us. Narcissism must be identified as the enemy of civilized life for individuals, families, society, and humanity. Chaos is the antithesis of civilization. The degree to which we emerge from a state of individual narcissism will determine the level of development with which we can relate to our families, society, and humanity. It is essential for each of us as individuals to grow up psychologically if we are to be equipped to relate to each other in a civilized manner. Chaos is the natural environment of the narcissist—no rules, no regulations, no demands, no responsibilities. It is the world that is appropriate only to the infant, a world of unconditional love and acceptance. If we are to be civilized, we must emerge from this world of chaos and distinguish self from other. We must establish our own boundaries so that we can respect the boundaries of our family members, society, and humanity. We must give up the regressive demand for unconditional love and acceptance and move forward developmentally to a place where rules are respected as the infrastructure of civilized life. We must insist on a meritocracy as the standard for advancement. We must know what we are striving to attain so that our strategies for achievement are clear. Individual and social efforts should be redirected to the goal of attaining self-sufficiency and responsible adulthood. Individual and social resources should be committed to this task. Underlying every decision regarding child-raising and social programs should be the standard of growth. "Does this decision encourage dependence or self-sufficiency?" Education is the vehicle for the transfer of information. We need to educate ourselves and constantly monitor our prog-ress by asking, "Who's driving the bus?" We must commit ourselves to objective reality, staying in the present, and being personally responsible for our behavior regardless of our state of mind. We need to demand from ourselves and from our leaders in society that responsible adults are in charge. We need a survivor's mentality. Dear America, we must grow up psychologically. We must defeat narcissism. We must choose life.

Happy New Year,
Linda Goudsmit

About the Author

 Linda Goudsmit is a devoted wife, mother, and grandmother. She and her husband have owned and operated a girls' clothing store in Michigan for forty years. Linda graduated from the University of Michigan in Ann Arbor, earning a B.A. in English literature. Having a lifelong commitment to learning, she is an avid reader and observer of life. It is with pride and humility that she is sharing her thoughts, observations, and philosophy of behavior in Dear America.

Acknowledgments

With affection and gratitude I acknowledge S.K. who first posed the question, "Who's driving the bus?"

With humility and admiration I acknowledge the brave thinkers, ancient and modern, who had the courage to express their thoughts for others to consider: Socrates, Plato, Aristotle, Nietzsche, Sigmund Freud, Kahlil Gibran, Erich Fromm, Ayn Rand, Hermann Hesse, Alice Miller, Eric Berne, Thomas A. Harris, John E. Sarno, Lee Harris, Harriet Goldhor Lerner, Steven and Sybil Wolin, E. James Anthony, Lois Barclay Murphy, Lloyd deMause, Mary Pipher, Stanton E. Samenow, Don Dinkmeyer, Gary D. McKay, and Dorothy Otnow Lewis. The study of human behavior is an ongoing multi-faceted conversation that will continue as long as people have the freedom to speak and the liberty to record their thoughts.

Index

Abusive parenting, 104

Addiction, 75, 77-78, 84-85, 87-88, 115, 117, 119, 121-122, 124-126, 129, 131, 133, 139-140, 142-144

Blame, 40, 42, 55, 57, 104, 114, 123-125, 150-151, 159, 163, 166

Bullies, 63

Causal Connection, 84, 86-87

Chaos, 52, 54, 58, 63-64, 148, 177-178

Child-raising, 37, 178

Childhood Trauma, 84-87, 125-126, 130, 133, 139-141, 143

Chronological Age, 14, 49, 59, 61, 114, 134-135

Civil War II, 13, 18, 25, 28, 44, 65, 69, 96, 98, 119-120, 163, 174

Civilized Society, 24-25, 27-28, 40, 47-49, 55, 57, 66, 69, 107-108, 123, 165, 167-168, 172-173

Competence, 153, 155

Criminals, 45, 51, 56, 106

Death, 14-15, 62, 73, 76, 89, 130, 148, 161

Denying, 108, 118, 129, 163

Dirty Harry, 46

Divorce, 73, 80-81, 84, 94-95, 161

Drugs, 97, 115, 117, 121, 133, 143

Education, 38, 67, 90, 173, 176, 178

Entitlements, 167, 174

Ethical, 21, 23-24, 43

Excuses, 22, 40-41, 45-46, 48-49, 53, 57, 59, 124, 132, 159, 163, 165-166, 169-173

Gangs, 59, 61, 64

Golding, William, 60, 63, 134

Hallmark of Abuse, 142

Heredity, 78, 87, 125, 139, 143, 145-146

Incompetent parenting, 101, 104, 110

Invulnerable Children, 82

Judges, 45, 54-55, 163

Just Say No, 172

Juvenile, 51-52, 54

Killing, 83

Loss, 33, 77, 93, 121, 140, 161

Merit-based, 153, 155

Narcissistic Adult, 25-27, 30, 56, 144, 152-153

Narcissistic Parent, 29-31, 38

Political, 41-43, 45, 64, 150

Politicians, 42-43, 45, 97, 150

Powerlessness, 85, 124-125, 141, 150

Private Sector, 53, 95

Psychiatrists, 40

Psychological Development, 9, 15, 31, 53, 59, 61, 64, 71, 110, 114, 159, 164

Psychological Growth, 14-15, 20, 39, 64, 70, 83, 87-88, 91, 96, 101, 104-105, 109, 112, 116-117, 123-124, 132, 135, 137, 147-148, 151, 164

Psychotherapy, 38, 91-92, 130, 160, 173

Public Sector, 53, 95

Rape, 46, 51, 83

Recovery, 129-130, 137-138

Reenactments, 73-75, 80, 82-84, 86-87, 89, 98, 108, 151

Regaining Control, 152

Regression, 18, 31, 42, 49, 53, 61-62, 115-117, 124, 147-148, 150, 161, 175

Religious, 97, 150-151

Repetition, 73, 85, 105

Repressing, 129

Resistance, 64, 109, 116-117, 130

Responsible Adult, 14-15, 19-21, 25-27, 33, 35, 38, 40, 55, 57-58, 60, 69, 91-93, 96, 99, 104, 109, 113, 122-124, 147, 149-152, 157, 170, 174

Responsible Leadership, 147

Responsible Parent, 29-30, 33, 176

Reunification, 121

Rudeness, 72

Rules, 24-27, 52, 54, 60, 63, 69, 177-178

Self, 14, 18, 27, 35, 57, 74, 76, 83, 98, 101, 117, 119, 121, 124, 129, 132, 135-136, 143-144, 149, 153-154, 171, 174, 178

Self-awareness, 38, 133, 151, 171

Self-knowledge, 123, 125, 132-133, 135-136, 142-143, 173, 176

Self-monitoring, 164, 174-175

Self-reunification, 121

Self-sufficiency, 15, 30, 37, 53, 90, 92, 100, 147, 166, 177-178

Separation, 62

Social Structures, 45

Sociologists, 40, 97, 150

Spousal Abuse, 23, 134-135, 159

State-of-mind, 50-51

Suicide, 42, 73, 76-78, 80, 84, 130

Survival Mentality, 70, 89

Temporary insanity, 107

Time-Warping, 68-69, 84, 105, 107, 130, 162

Unconditional Love, 23-24, 97, 144, 172, 177-178

Victimization, 45, 48, 105, 160

Violence, 38, 58, 73, 83-85, 90, 117, 121, 124, 132-133, 141, 143

Wholeness, 115, 117, 121, 132

CPSIA information can be obtained
at www.ICGtesting.com
Printed in the USA
BVOW09s1800131117
500282BV00020B/572/P